## Praise for Sant Rajinder Singh's books

"Sant Rajinder Singh Ji explains how peace can be created through meditation and inner reflection. There will be no lasting peace unless individual human beings have some sense of inner peace. To create inner peace it is necessary to calm the mind, hence the importance of meditation. I greatly appreciate Sant Rajinder Singh Ji's contribution here to the goal of peace that we are all working towards. May readers of this book find peace within themselves through meditation and so foster a greater sense of peace throughout the world."

--H.H. the Dalai Lama

"This outstanding handbook reflects Rajinder Singh's deep wisdom and realization emerging from divine love and inner fulfillment."

--Deepak Chopra

"A powerful, deep, clearly written book about practical spirituality that helps us let go of the self-made blocks that interfere with the awareness that we are one with God and each other, that there is no separation, and that our soul is present and fully alive forever."

---Gerald G. Jampolsky, M.D.,
Author of *Love is Letting Go of Fear*

"Firmly rooted in traditional wisdom, the author faces contemporary questions and challenges squarely and in a non-sectarian way...to bring the seed of peace within us to fruition in daily life and the world we live in."

--Brother David-Steindl Rast

"Rajinder Singh's new book is food for the soul. It is an inspiring and informative source that speaks to both beginners and experienced travelers on the path of life. I was uplifted as I read this book, and re-dedicate myself to honoring my inner work."

---Educator, Recording Artist, and Musician, Steven Halpern

"Meditation empowers us in two spiritual arenas. First, it leads us to inner peace and fulfillment.... Second, meditation allows us to use our talents and skills to make the world a better place to live. Rajinder Singh ............ beautifully. He says that by mastering medi............ 'fillment, we become an instr............ hose around us."

itor, *Personal Transformation*

"...Rajinder .............. hat true peace and happiness can only come from within: the ...... in learning how to tap into them."

--Here's Health magazine

## Other Books by Sant Rajinder Singh

*Inner and Outer Peace through Meditation*
*(with a Foreword by H.H. the Dalai Lama)*
*Empowering Your Soul through Meditation*
*Spiritual Pearls for Enlightened Living*
*Silken Thread of the Divine*
*Echoes of the Divine*
*Spiritual Thirst*
*Education for a Peaceful World*
*Visions of Spiritual Unity and Peace*
*Ecology of the Soul and Positive Mysticism*
*Vision of the New Millennium*

### IN HINDI

*Spirituality in Modern Times*
*True Happiness*
*Self Realization*
*Search for Peace within the Soul*
*Salvation through Naam*
*Spiritual Treasures*
*Experience of the Soul*
*Spiritual Talks*

# Inner and Outer Peace through Meditation

Rajinder Singh

**Radiance Publishers**

**Radiance Publishers**
1042 Maple Ave. Lisle, IL 60532
Website: www.radiancepublishers.com
Email: sales@radiancepublishers.com

**Publishing History**
First published in the US by Element Books, Inc. 1996
Second published by Element, An Imprint of
HarperCollins*Publishers,* 2003
This edition published by Radiance Publishers, 2007


11 10 09 08  3 4 5 6 7 8 9 10


© **Copyright 2007 by Radiance Publishers**
**Text © 1996 SK Publications**

**Library of Congress Control Number: 2007923121**

**ISBN 978-0-918224-53-8**

This eBook edition published 2013

# Contents

## Part III  Outer Peace

Dedicated to my spiritual teachers,
Sant Kirpal Singh Ji Maharaj
and Sant Darshan Singh Ji Maharaj,
who shared with the world
a method of meditation
that can lead humanity
to inner and outer peace.

# Acknowledgments

I would like to acknowledge and thank my revered spiritual teachers, Sant Kirpal Singh Ji Maharaj (1894–1974) and Sant Darshan Singh Ji Maharaj (1921–1989), from whom I learned the practice of meditation. Sant Kirpal Singh Ji is known throughout the world today as the "Father of the Human Unity movement." Sant Darshan Singh Ji was recognized as one of the leading mystic poet-saints of modern times and received four Urdu Academy Awards for his poetry. The eternal values of life and the practical method of meditation that can be practiced by people of all ages, all nations, all religions, and all walks of life that they taught me, I pass along to humanity in this book.

I would also like to acknowledge my revered mother, Mata Harbhajan Kaur Ji, who stood by the side of my father in his spiritual work, and who has been an inspiration to me.

I would like to thank my dear wife, Rita Ji, who works tirelessly and selflessly to serve humanity and to spread love to people all over the world, knitting people together as a part of one large family.

I would like to also thank Jay and Ricki Linksman for their help in seeing this manuscript through to publication.

And I would like to thank God, for His love, grace, and countless bounties. May His Light and love illuminate every heart.

Rajinder Singh

# Foreword

In this book Sant Rajinder Singh Ji Maharaj explains how peace can be created through meditation and inner reflection.

I believe that the very purpose of life is to be happy. From the moment of birth, every human being wants happiness and does not want suffering. From the very core of our being, we simply desire contentment. Therefore, it is important to discover what will bring about the greatest degree of happiness. When we consider what we human beings really are, we find we are not like machine-made objects. Therefore, it is a mistake to place all our hopes for happiness on external development alone. Hence, we should devote our most serious efforts to bringing about mental peace.

It is my experience that the greatest degree of inner tranquility comes from the development of love and compassion. The more we care for the happiness of others, the greater is our own sense of well-being. Cultivating a close, warm-hearted feeling for others automatically puts the mind at ease.

In pursuit of global peace we may talk about demilitarization, but to begin with some kind of inner disarmament is necessary. The key to genuine world peace is inner peace, and the foundation of that is a sense of understanding and respect for each other as human beings, based on compassion and love. Compassion is, by nature, peaceful and gentle, but it is also very powerful. It is a sign of true inner strength. Nevertheless, compassion does not arise simply by ordering it to do so. Such a sincere feeling must grow gradually, cultivated within each individual, based on their own conviction of its worth.

There will be no lasting world peace unless individual human beings have some sense of inner peace. To create inner peace it is necessary to calm the mind, hence the importance of meditation. I greatly appreciate Sant Rajinder Singh Ji Maharaj's contribution here to the goal of peace that we are all working towards. May readers of this book find peace within themselves through meditation and so foster a greater sense of peace throughout the world.

The Dalai Lama

# PART I

# Inner Peace

# Meditation for Inner Peace

WE LIVE IN AN AGE in which we have made tremendous progress in the areas of science and technology. We have sent spacecraft to the moon and the planets in our solar system and have investigated the particles of the subatomic world. Great strides have been made in the medical arena. Scientists and doctors have found cures for many illnesses and can even replace vital body organs to keep a patient alive. The vast array of inventions and gadgets should have provided humanity with happiness and peace. Yet with all the advanced technology, we are not at peace. There is something missing in our lives. We find people in our times plagued by continual stress and tension. Stress-related illnesses have been on the rise. Many people have interpersonal problems and are unhappy in their relationships.

We find conflict at the level of the family, the community, the nation, and the world.

People try a variety of means to escape the pains and disappointments of life. Some try to find happiness by visiting places of entertainment or through engaging in sensual pleasures. Many turn to drugs or alcohol. All these means of escape may provide some momentary or temporary happiness, but they are not cures. We still must return to face the problems of life. Some of these means of escape are even addictive or harmful. In this age of scientific advances we begin to wonder if there is a way to find lasting happiness in this world. Is fulfillment possible, or is it only a dream?

Many of the greatest thinkers, philosophers, saints, mystics, and founders of religions have spent their lives in pursuit of permanent and lasting peace and happiness. If we read the writings of saints and mystics throughout the ages, we find that they discovered that true happiness and peace lie within us.

In the past few decades we find more and more people coming to the same conclusion as did the saints and mystics of the past: people are exploring meditation as a means to find peace and happiness within themselves. Recent studies in the field of science are confirming that meditation can improve our physical and mental well-being. Besides having a positive effect on our body and mind, it also helps us develop spiritually. Thus, meditation can help us in the physical, mental, and spiritual spheres of our lives.

Meditation is being prescribed by doctors and specialists as a treatment for a number of stress-related ailments, such as heart disease, breathing difficulties, and stomach problems. One medical study by Dr. John L. Craven published in the *Canadian Journal of Psychiatry* states: "Controlled studies have found consistent reductions in anxiety in meditators ... Several stress-related conditions have demonstrated improvement during clinical trials of meditation including: hypertension, insomnia, asthma, chronic pain, cardiac tachyarrhythmias, phobic anxiety." (Craven, Dr. John L., "Meditation and Psychotherapy," *Canadian Journal of Psychiatry*, Vol. 34, October 1989, pp. 648–53).

Many hospitals and medical centers have begun to offer courses in meditation to help their patients improve their health. Meditation helps the body in several ways. It puts us into a relaxed state. In another study, Dr. Ilan Kutz states:

> As the ability to meditate develops, a hierarchy of sensations develops, ranging from deep relaxation to marked emotional and cognitive alterations ... The altered physiological mechanisms by which emotions and cognitions are altered due to meditation have not been completely delineated ... Many of these peripheral changes are compatible with decreased arousal of the sympathetic nervous system ... The peripheral physiological changes have proven to be of value as a primary or adjunctive treatment for a variety of medical disorders such as hypertension and cardiac arrhythmias, as well as in relieving anxiety states and pain. (Kutz, MD, Ilan, *et al.*, "Meditation and Psychotherapy," *American Journal of Psychiatry*, Vol. 142, January 1985, pp. 1–8).

While in meditation we forget the body. Our limbs and

body become totally relaxed. While fully concentrated in meditation, we even lose awareness of any pain or discomfort in our body. The more time we spend in meditation, the more time our body remains relaxed. It is said that one hour of complete concentration in meditation is equal to four hours of sleep. Thus in our busy life, putting in time for meditation has the effect of several hours rest. We come out of the meditation with renewed strength and vitality.

Meditation is also being used to reduce a variety of problems that affect people mentally and emotionally. Though science has helped us to master our physical environment, many people find themselves without any control over situations that arise around them. We find that people have a host of problems dealing with their interpersonal relationships. They are troubled by anxiety, depression, anger, fear, lack of self-esteem, and a variety of other emotional conditions. A large segment of the population takes alcohol and a variety of drugs to alleviate their mental and emotional pain. Meditation provides a solution which is safe, effective, and lasting.

In meditation we come in contact with a divine power. This power manifests itself as a loving light. When we contact this light within ourselves, we experience a profound peace, bliss, and happiness unlike any we can find in this world. We are permeated with a divine love which engulfs and fulfills us. There is so much joy within us that we do not want to leave that state. The beauty of meditation is that this intoxication remains with us even after we resume our daily activities.

Meditation does not eliminate the problems of life, but

we look at them from a new angle of vision. There is an instructive story from the life of Akbar the Great of India. Akbar was an emperor and he had a court of advisors. The wisest of his counselors was Birbal. One day, Akbar posed a problem to his counselors to see who could solve it. He drew a line in the sand with a stick and asked who could shorten the line without touching any part of it. The counselors scratched their heads not knowing what to do. They could not imagine how a line could be shortened without rubbing it away or touching it. But Birbal stepped forward, picked up a stick, and drew a longer line parallel to the first, thus making the first one look shorter.

Meditation provides a similar solution to the problems of life: it does not eliminate them, but it gives us a new angle of vision, a new perspective. It takes us above the sphere of the physical world so we can enter regions of peace and bliss. Contact with this inner intoxication is so fulfilling that we no longer look at problems of this world in the same light. They begin to dissipate as vaporous bubbles. We carry this inner ecstasy with us and can tap into it anytime we wish. This inner bliss helps us to become oblivious to our pains and sorrows. We realize there is more to life than this physical world. When we realize that our life in this world is but a temporary stay of fifty, sixty, or a hundred years, and that there is a life beyond, a higher reality, the problems of life do not seem to affect us as much. We recognize that the little idiosyncrasies of other people, the difficulties that bother us in our jobs, homes, or neighborhoods, are as passing storms, and we know that there is a realm of blue, clear skies filled with radiant Light shining above the clouds.

On another level, meditation helps us to increase our powers of concentration and our efficiency in our mundane spheres. By regularly practicing meditation, we become used to controlling our attention. We then can direct our attention to focus on anything we wish, such as our studies, our careers, our sports, our art, or in solving problems. We become used to focusing on one thing at a time. This concentrated effort helps us excel in any area we choose. Success in any sphere is a result of sustained effort and con-centrated attention. We develop this quality through con-tinually practicing meditation. Thus, besides the physical and mental benefits of meditation, our outer circumstances improve due to the increased success we gain in our outer life.

Traditionally, meditation has been the means by which people developed themselves spiritually. Whether it is called concentration, inversion, prayer, or meditation, each religion and philosophy speaks of it as a way to gain knowledge of our soul and of the divine power within us. For ages, humanity has wondered about questions such as who we are, from where did we come, to where do we go when we die, and is there God. Both science and religion have sought to answer these questions. The process of meditation is one that gives us an experiential knowledge of the beyond and provides answers to these questions.

Through meditation we are able to separate our soul from the body and journey in the beyond. We hear of people who have had near-death experiences who upon the clinical death of their body passed through a tunnel. They emerged into a region of Light and met a being of radiant Light. They experienced so much love, warmth, and peace from this being that they had never had in their physical lives. They realized that they had an existence which outlasted their physical bodies. Through meditation we can have this experience without having to undergo a clinical death. We can easily, gently, and naturally rise above our body, experience the regions of bliss, Light, and beauty beyond, and discover our own immortality.

By exploring the inner realms, we learn what happens after death. The spiritual journey actually begins where the near-death experiences end. We discover the beauty, love, and eternal peace within ourselves. Once we see this higher reality, we see this world as merely a temporary home. By separating our soul from the body, we lose the fear of death. We journey into spiritual regions filled with so much ecstasy that we do not even wish to return to this world. Thus, we know that higher realms await us and that death is not the end of our existence.

Meditation helps us attain inner peace. When our soul contacts the Light beyond, we are filled with a total tranquility and fulfillment. We become at peace with ourselves and are not bothered by problems around us. This peace radiates to all who come in contact with us. Thus we become a source of joy and inspiration for others, whether it be our family members, our friends and relations, our co-workers, our society, or the world.

One of the benefits of achieving inner peace is that it contributes to outer peace in the world. When we rise above our physical body and experience ourselves as soul, we also see that all other beings are also souls. We see that the same Light that is within us is within everyone else. We start to realize that we are all souls, all part of God. We are all members of one family. When we see our essential unity, we begin to develop love for all. When we love others as if they were members of our own family, we feel a desire to help them. We do not want to see anyone in pain. Thus, we become nonviolent and peaceful. We care about all living things and our environment. We begin to have a positive influence on others in our environment.

If each person attains inner peace through meditation and develops love for all, it will not be long before peace prevails on our planet. We will live in unity and harmony with each other. In this way, our personal attainment of peace and happiness will contribute to a golden age of peace and happiness on earth.

# Attaining Spiritual Consciousness

*A*s our eyes open to the light of the dawning millennium, we see before us vistas of new realities. The world we see before us is vastly altered from the world of yesterday. Far more dramatic than the changes brought about by technology are the changes in our perception of the world. Science has broadened our vision to extend from the minutest subatomic particles to the brilliant light radiating from distant quasars. The universe is no longer perceived as solid matter, but dancing packets of ever-whirling energy. Our world view has shifted from believing in only what one can perceive with the five senses to recognizing that there is more than what we see with our physical eyes.

Science has begun to enter previously forbidden realms to explore dimensions not measurable by ordinary instru-

ments. Scientists are awakening to the existence of pheno-
mena that cannot be explained by antiquated science textbooks with their limited perspective. In discovering that
there are dimensions beyond this physical one they are
changing our concept of reality. Journals abound with
hypotheses about the origin of our universe, about black
holes of minute size containing tremendous energy, about
the possibility of entering space at one point and emerging
in a far distant galaxy. What previously was material for
science fiction writers is now the basis of serious study.

Besides exploring outer space, scientists have begun researching the realm of inner space. We find medical doctors
reporting cases of people who had near-death experiences
in which they underwent clinical death yet were revived.
Dr. Raymond Moody's book, *Life After Life*, documents
cases in which people who underwent the near-death experience reported similar experiences. In the interim period
while they were declared dead many reported leaving the
body and finding themselves floating in the room, looking
down at their physical body. They could float through the
hospital, oftentimes seeing their relatives in the other
room and listening to their conversations. A remarkable
number of people experienced soaring through a tunnel to
a region of Light where they met a benign, radiant being.
They experienced a transcendent peace and happiness,
which they found difficult to leave. Even children whose
lives were restored following a clinical death described this
same experience. The number of people who underwent
these near-death experiences is so large and the descriptions so strikingly similar that doctors and scientists find it
difficult to ignore the possibility that there is more to who

we are than our physical body. All who have undergone such an experience came to the same conclusion: There is life beyond our present life.

These findings are corroborated with the experiences of mystics throughout the ages. What seems new to the Western mind has been widely accepted knowledge for centuries in the East. In each religion we find accounts of similar experiences in which one's consciousness can be separated from the physical body. We find extraordinary descriptions of higher states of consciousness in different religions. In Hinduism, we find the ancient story of Savitri, whose husband was taken from her by death. Savitri is said to have left the body, apprehending the angel of death and imploring him to return her husband to life. Such was the power of her love, that her husband was revived. In Buddhism, we have the *Tibetan Book of the Dead*, that describes in detail the journey of the soul as it departs from this world. Islam describes in detail regions of heaven, hell, and *ahraf* (purgatory) to which a soul passes after this physical existence is over. In Christianity we have the book of Revelations, rich in description of realms beyond this world. In the *Kabbalah* of Judaism, a cosmogony of higher planes is described.

A deeper study into the heart of each religion reveals a wealth of mystic experiences described by the saints and spiritual adepts. Each in its own time has taught disciples how to transcend physical consciousness and explore spiritual realms.

Spiritual consciousness is our birthright. It is the highest attainment we can achieve in our lifetime. We may have thought that these states were the monopoly of saints, but the experimentation of modern scientists and mystics confirms that the average person may also enjoy spiritual consciousness. There are simple steps to spiritual consciousness. Unbounded joy, happiness, and inner peace await us when we discover the freedom, the exhilaration, and the wonder of enlightenment that comes from attaining spiritual consciousness.

What is spiritual consciousness? It is becoming conscious of the soul and God within us. Most of us are aware of our body, of the thoughts passing through our mind, and of the world around us. This is called body or physical consciousness. But we are more than our body and mind. We are actually a soul, a conscious entity which inhabits the body. The soul is a part of the Oversoul, whether we call it God, the Creator, Allah, Wah-i-Guru, or Parmatma. It is of the same essence as God. The soul is what enlivens the body. When the soul leaves the body at the time of death, the body dies. But the soul does not die. It is immortal. Just as people who clinically died experienced a continued existence outside their body, so will each of us continue to exist even after the demise of our mortal frame. This consciousness at the level of soul, independent of our body and mind, is what is termed spiritual consciousness.

We do not have to wait until our physical end to know what it is like perceiving life at the level of soul. It is an experience many have enjoyed during their lifetimes and is available to every human being. We have read in the scriptures of various religions about people who had experienced spiritual consciousness. Buddha attained enlightenment under the bodhi tree. St. Paul said, "I live; not now I, but Christ lives in me." Baha'u'llah, the mystic saint of

Persia, said, "O Son of dust! hearken unto the mystic voice calling from the realm of the Invisible ... up from thy prison, ascend unto the glorious meadows above and from thy mortal cage wing thy flight unto the paradise of the Placeless."

These inner experiences are not limited to peoples of antiquity. Anyone in our own time who wishes to develop this for him- or herself may have such experiences and verify the reality of the soul. The steps to spiritual consciousness are simple and can be practiced by people of all religions, all nationalities, and all walks of life. The method is available for all those who wish to discover the treasure of their soul and the infinite consciousness, joy, peace, and bliss latent within.

The first step to spiritual consciousness is learning the art of meditation. The next step is to achieve personal transformation so we can lead a life in the world that increases our spiritual consciousness. It involves living life in such a way that our consciousness remains centered in our soul while we are attending to our worldly duties and responsibilities. This means that we develop spiritual qualities such as nonviolence, truthfulness, purity, humility, and selfless service. Finally, inner peace and personal transformation lead to outer peace in the world. By attaining inner peace, we can make a positive contribution to human unity, universal love, and the improvement of all life on this planet.

Meditation is the method used throughout the ages to re-identify with our soul. It is a process of inverting our attention from the outer world and the body to focus on the doorway leading to spiritual dimensions. It is our soul that can gain entrance to this inner kingdom. When we identify ourselves with our true essence we will be able to traverse realms of wonder within. We will discover the wealth of spiritual regions rich in knowledge modern science can only dream about. Spiritual consciousness is actually all-consciousness. It is awareness of everything there is to be known. It is like tapping into a master computer network in which all knowledge is programmed. Through meditation we gain access to this infinite source of wisdom.

# THREE

# Meditation on the Inner Light and Sound

---

*I*f we examine the ideas that occupy the impossible dreams of humanity today, we will gain insight into what may become possibilities of tomorrow. With technological and scientific know-how advancing at a dizzying rate, the future is closer than we think.

Science, in its attempt to explore the farthest reaches of space, is looking for answers to the origin of creation. In their quest, they inevitably have had to cross the barriers of science and enter a realm previously reserved for only mystics, philosophers, and enlightened saints. Scientists have accepted the limitations of current scientific tools in helping them reach back in time to understand what happened before the theoretical Big Bang that set our universe in motion. Many physicists have turned to the East to explore the possibilities of realms of existence beyond the physical universe. A look at New Age physics reveals a generation of scientists who are exploring the possibility that there really are universes existing concurrently with ours.

While these ideas may seem far-fetched to hard-core skeptics, increasing numbers of people have opened their minds to the possibility that there is more going on in creation than what meets the physical eye.

History has proven that the visionary thinking of scientists and thinkers of the past, which were scoffed at by their contemporaries, have come to pass. Hundreds of years ago, when Leonardo da Vinci sketched his ideas for a flying machine, people thought it was more a "flight of his imagination" than anything else. When the movie moguls of the first half of this century produced epics of spaceships traveling at supersonic speeds, it was labeled as science fiction. When early dreamers designed machines that could "think" for human beings, they were considered as visions of a future that might or might not be possible. Yet today we see that airplanes, spaceships, and computers are no longer science fiction, but science fact.

Modern humanity at large has learned the lesson that anything is possible. While science is delving into what happens after this life, there is another field of science also being researched which is investigating whether higher regions of existence can be tapped during this current lifetime. Through the science of spirituality people are actively engaged in exploring other realms of existence. Spiritual teachers, saints, and mystics have developed a technique by which one can transcend the physical limitations of this universe to discover higher realms of consciousness. When they refer to higher realms of consciousness they are not referring to brain wave states of alpha, beta, or theta; they are not referring to altered states of consciousness which can be induced by mind-altering drugs; they are referring to actual places and regions to which we can travel by transcending this restricted physical plane through a process known as meditation on the inner Light and Sound. Through meditation, one can explore higher planes and verify the truth of their existence for ourselves.

Meditation is the process by which we withdraw our attention from the world outside and our body and concentrate it at a point between and behind the two eyebrows. By focusing our attention there, we come in contact with a current of Light and Sound which will lead us from our physical consciousness into higher consciousness, into the Beyond.

৺

## Light and Sound

I would like to share with you what the great saints, mystics, and spiritual teachers have said about the Light and Sound of God, the regions beyond, and then describe the method of meditation they use to journey there. This spiritual science is not new. It has been at the heart of every religion. References to the Light and Sound, and the realms Beyond, can be found in the scriptures of the major religions.

In Sikhism, Guru Nanak states:
*All knowledge and meditation sprang from Dhun (the
  principle of Light and Sound),
But what That is, defies definition.*

The Sufi mystic, Maulana Rumi, has said:
> *Rising above the horizon, hearken to the Melody Divine,*
> *The Prophet would attend to It as to any other task.*

The Muslim mystic, Shah Niaz, says:
> *O God, lead me to the place from where flows the ineffable*
> *Kalma without words.*

There are two sides to every religion: the exoteric or outer teachings, and the esoteric or inner teachings. The esoteric side deals with exploration of the Beyond. Saints and founders of the various religions had themselves traveled to higher realms and taught the method of going within to their followers. With time, the inner teachings, usually conveyed by word of mouth from teacher to student, have been lost. Only the outer teachings, which carry allegorical references to the inner side, remain. Throughout the ages, there have always been enlightened souls who revived and imparted the esoteric teachings. Each of them have described the inner journey. While the language in which they spoke differed, the experiences described are the same.

Guru Arjan Dev has said:
> *The All-pervading Music is going on everywhere,*
> *In the heart of all, the Divine Music flows.*

St. John has said:
> *And the light shineth in darkness; and the darkness*
> *comprehendeth it not.*

In the Old Testament it is said:
> *Thy Word is a Lamp unto my feet, and a Light unto my*
> *path.*

Kabir has said:
> *The tuneful trumpet of Thy doorway,*

*Sounds in the middle of my forehead.*

Mohammed has said:

*The Voice of God comes unto my ears as any other sounds.*

Guru Nanak has said:

*Within the heavenly Light and from it Bani or Sound doth proceed,*
*And it doth attune the soul with the true Lord.*

This Light and Sound is the creative vibration which emanated from God which brought all creation into being. Religions have referred to it by various names. In the ancient Hindu scriptures it is called *Nad, Udgit, Anhad Shabd*, or *Jyoti* or *Sruti*. In the *Hansa Naad Upanishad* it is written:

*Meditation on Nad or the Sound Principle is the royal road to salvation.*

The Buddhists called it Sonorous Light. In the *Tibetan Book of the Dead* (*Bardo Thodol*), edited by Dr. W.Y. Evans-Wentz (London, 1957) it is written:

O nobly-born, when thy body and mind were separating thou must have experienced a glimpse of Pure Truth, subtle, sparkling, bright, dazzling, glorious, and radiantly awesome, in appearance like a mirage moving across a landscape in springtime in one continuous stream of vibrations. Be not daunted thereby, nor terrified, nor awed. That is the radiance of thine own true nature. Recognize it. From the midst of that radiance, the natural sound of Reality, reverberating like a thousand thunders simultaneously sounding, will come. That is the natural sound of thine own real self. Be not daunted thereby, nor terrified, nor awed.

The Greek philosophers called it *Logos* or the Music of the Spheres. In the Bible it is referred to as *the Word*: "In the beginning was the Word, and the Word was with God, and the Word was God." (John 1:1). In the Psalms it is written: "By the Word of the Lord were the heavens made; and all the host of them ... He spake and it was done; he commanded, and it stood fast." (Psalm 33: 6, 9). The Muslims refer to it as *Kalma*. Hazrat Bahu has said:

> *All repeat the Kalma by word of mouth,*
> *A rare soul may do so with the tongue of thought.*
> *He who communes with it mentally, he can hardly describe*
> *    it in words.*

The Sufis call it *Baang-e-Asmani, Baang-e-Ilahi,* or *Saut-e-Sarmadi*. The Zoroastrians call it *Sraosha* or the Creative Verbum: "I cause to invoke that divine Sraosha (the Word) which is the greatest of all divine gifts for spiritual succor."

The Sikhs called it *Naam* or *Shabd*. In the *Jap Ji* it is said:

> *There is one Reality, the Unmanifest Manifested;*
> *Ever-existent, He is Naam (Conscious Spirit);*
> *The Creator pervading all;*
> *Without fear, without enmity; The Timeless, the Unborn*
> *    and the Self-existent, Complete within Itself.*

The Light and Sound is the creative power that brought all the various regions into existence. It created the physical universe, earth, human beings, and all other forms of life. This Power of God which flows out from God also returns to Him. When the soul is withdrawn to a point known as the seat of the soul, it can then travel on the Light and Sound through the higher planes, back to its Source, in the purely spiritual realm. The process by which the soul is brought into contact with the current of Light and Sound reverberating within us is called meditation.

❧

## Contacting the Light through Our Attention

The reason we are not aware of the Light and Sound within is due to our attention. The outer expression of the soul is known as the attention. Presently, our attention is scattered throughout our body and goes out of our body into this world through the five senses: seeing, hearing, smell, taste, and touch. We have to withdraw our attention from the world outside and collect it at the seat of the soul, located between and behind the two eyebrows. This point is referred to in different scriptures as the single eye, the third eye, the tenth door or *daswan dwar*, the *divya chakshu*, or the *ajna chakra*. Meditation, pure and simple, is the withdrawing of our attention from the outer world and the focusing of it at the third eye. This is the point at which we concentrate our attention in order to see the inner Light and hear the Celestial Sound.

Some forms of yoga deal with controlling the bodily functions. In our body we have two currents. We have the motor currents and the sensory currents which are flowing through our bodies. The motor currents keep us alive, by controlling our involuntarily body functions, such as the growth of our nails and hair, our breathing, and our blood circulation. In meditation on the inner Light and Sound, one does not practice the control of the motor currents for transcending the body. The motor currents are allowed to go on by themselves so that the process by which we survive in this world is not tampered with. Instead, we withdraw the sensory currents. The sensory currents give us sensation in the body. It is the sensory currents which make us aware of the sense of sight, hearing, smell, taste, and touch. It is through the senses that we enjoy seeing beautiful sights, hearing pleasing sounds, smelling sweet fragrances, tasting delicious foods, and having pleasurable sensations through the sense of touch. If we withdraw our sensory currents from the outside world, and collect them at the eye-focus, we will be able to see and hear with the inner eye and ear, and travel to the realms within.

This is the same process that we undergo at the time of death. When someone dies, there is numbness first in their feet. Then, the numbness continues to their legs and trunk. Finally, their soul collects at the eye-focus. At the time of their death we find their eyeballs turn up, and then come down. So the soul is collecting and leaving the body. In meditation on the inner Light and Sound, the point of concentration used is the third eye as this is the highest *chakra* in the body. It is the point from where the soul leaves the body at the time of death.

There are six *chakras* or centers in the body. There is the *guda chakra* located at the base of the spine or the rectum. There is the *indri chakra* located near the reproductive organs. There is the *nabhi chakra* located near the navel. There is the *hriday chakra* found near the heart. The *kanth chakra* is located near the throat. The *ajna* or *aggya chakra* is known as the third eye or tenth door, and is located between and behind the two eyebrows. Since the soul has to pass through all these *chakras* in order to leave the body in meditation, we need to concentrate at the highest point, the last *chakra* which the soul must pass before leaving the body. When life is so short and we have only a limited amount of time available to us, why spend it trying to reach the lower *chakras*, and then moving from one to the next, when in that same amount of time we can go right to the highest point. Thus, we should start our concentration at the highest point so we can reach the goal faster.

Meditation is in reality a process of concentration. It does not need any *asanas* or difficult postures or any rigorous physical activity. It is so simple and natural that it can be practiced by a young child or an elderly person, or by someone who has some physical disability. Every human being can have access to the inner realms through the simple process of meditation.

**Note to the Reader:** In each of the following chapters, there are exercises to help apply in one's daily life the concepts presented throughout the book.

## EXERCISE

Sit quietly and observe your awareness. Are you aware of your body and its sensations? Are you aware of your environment? Are you aware of other people? Are you aware of your thoughts? Realize that awareness of your body, your environment, and your thoughts is called "body-consciousness."

Now, sit quietly again and focus your attention on your single or third eye. Try to stay focused there without any awareness of your body, your environment, and your thoughts. See how long you can keep your mind free of any distracting thoughts. This is the first step in meditation or concentration. It is the beginning of the withdrawal of your attention from the world to the still point at the third eye. In the next chapter you will learn the meditation practice.

# FOUR

# Meditation Instructions

---

ﻉ

## Step One: Finding a Time and Place for Meditation

*I*t is best to find a time and place in which we will have the least distractions from our environment. We should choose a time and place in which we will not be disturbed by phone calls and there is quietude in the atmosphere. That is why the time between three and six o'clock in the morning is recommended. In India this time is referred to as *amrit vela* or *Brahm mahulab* because that is the quietest time of the day. But in this day and age, that is not a necessity. We can meditate at any time in which we will not be disturbed. As we develop our concentration, we should be able to meditate even in a noisy environment. But to help us in the beginning, it is definitely preferable to sit in an area in which there will not be any noise, any telephones ringing, or any outside activity. Once we have perfected our inner travels, then we can meditate anywhere we like. In the beginning, however, it definitely helps if the surroundings are conducive to sitting for meditation.

We should sit in meditation only at times when we are fully awake. If we try to sit in meditation when we have just come back from work and are tired, then chances are that in that process we will fall asleep. So we want to find a time which is most suitable for us, during which we are fully awake and relaxed.

The main point is that we can meditate whenever we find the right time and right place for ourselves.

### ❧

## Step Two: Selecting a Pose

We should sit in a pose which is most convenient to us. This could be at any place in our house. We do not have to leave our house to meditate. Meditation can be practiced anywhere. We can sit on a chair, we can sit on the floor, we can sit on a sofa, we can sit cross-legged or with legs straight. We can sit in any manner. One can even meditate standing up or lying down. The main thing is to meditate wherever we are comfortable. The only thing that is expected of us is that whatever pose we choose should be one in which we can be still for the longest period of time. Before the mind can be stilled, the body has to be stilled. We want to be sure that in whatever pose we select, we can remain without moving, shaking, or scratching an itch. For those who are physically unable to sit, they can even lie down. The reason lying down is not recommended is that it is conducive to falling asleep.

In whatever pose we adopt, there should be no tension in any part of the body. We should sit in a relaxed pose. Once we select the pose, we should not change it during that meditation sitting. We should remain physically still.

**ೞ**

## Step Three: Concentrating

Once we pick a pose, we should close our eyes very gently, just as we do when going to sleep, and concentrate on seeing what lies in front of us. There should be no pressure on the eyes. Our eyes should be as relaxed as they are when we go to sleep. Since these physical eyes are not those by which we will be seeing the inner realms, there is no need to turn our eyeballs upwards in the hopes that we will see something there. We should not concentrate on the forehead. Instead, we should keep our eyeballs horizontal, as if we were looking straight ahead.

If the eyeballs look or turn upwards, we will feel a little pressure on the forehead, which may result in two problems. We may get a headache or we may generate heat in that area and our forehead will become hot. That will create problems for us which will cause us to move or get up to do something to cool ourselves down. That will interrupt our meditation. So we need to focus our attention a few inches in front of us.

When we close our eyes we will first see darkness. That which sees the darkness is our inner eye. With the inner eye, we should gaze lovingly, sweetly, and penetratingly into whatever is in front of us. We should be relaxed but attentive, as if we were watching a movie screen and waiting for the movie to begin. This is a process in which we do not worry about the world outside or what is going on in the body below. We are only trying to invert so as to reach the worlds within.

❧

## Step Four: Silencing Thought

Once we close our eyes and focus our attention in front of us, the mind will distract our concentration with thoughts. Our mind is like mercury, always restless and moving about. We will start thinking about all our problems. We will think about the past, we will think about the present, and we will think about the future. It could bring us thoughts about our work, about our families, or about our friends. Mind has many ways of trying to distract us from sitting in meditation and of keeping us from learning about our soul and God.

In our body we have our soul and our mind. The mind is a powerful entity whose main aim is to keep the soul in the body so that it does not reach the inner realms. The mind will try to keep our attention entangled in the physical world. It will do its best to prevent us from rising above this physical body and returning to God. The mind will keep us constantly thinking of our problems at work or at home. It will engage us in continually making plans for the future. We need to realize the soul is our real self; it is the part of us that is of the same essence as God. Unfortunately we have been separated from God. If we can realize that our soul is covered by the mind and body, and understand that the mind's role is to keep us from knowing our soul, we will be better able to still our mind.

For perfect concentration, we have to reach a state where there are no thoughts. If we have any thoughts, whether they are good or bad, they are all bad for us as far as meditation is concerned. Thoughts are like chains. The iron chains are our bad thoughts. But even if good thoughts are chains of gold, they are still chains. Thus, good thoughts are still distractions and will not help us in the process of meditation.

To provide assistance to help us bring our attention to the eye-focus and to still the mind, we should repeat any names of God with which we feel comfortable. The mind is a great distraction and keeps the attention from concentrating at the seat of the soul. However, if the mind is busy in the repetition of these names, it cannot distract the attention with thoughts. While we gaze into the middle of what lies in front of us, we repeat the names. The names are to be repeated mentally, with the tongue of thought, not out loudly. They are to be repeated slowly, at intervals, not in quick succession. There should be a slight pause between each Name.

❧

## Step Five: Concentrating on the Inner Light and Sound

We need to realize the Light within us. It is like having a light bulb. If you put four or five sheaths over it, pretty soon you will not see the light from the bulb. So this process of concentration, this process of meditation, is one by which we try to remove these sheaths one by one. We try to go within so that we can see the Light within us. Once we see how much illumination there is within, we will automatically want to see more and more of it. We will want to be in that state all the time. Similarly, unless we once taste the bliss of contacting the Light within, we cannot appreciate it. But once we go within, we crave that enjoyment more and more.

There are two meditation practices. The first is concentration on the inner Light. During this practice the repetition of the Names continues. This repetition is called *simran*. While the repetition goes on mentally we gaze at the field of darkness lying in front of us. We should not think about the world outside, the body below, or the process of withdrawal of the sensory currents from the body. We should not put attention on our breathing. Our breathing should go on normally, just as it does when we read, study, work, or move about. As we go about our day-to-day life we do not think about our breathing. Similarly, in meditation it should go on automatically.

Our job is to sit calmly and quietly and lovingly gaze into the darkness lying in front of us. As we do so, the attention will automatically begin to collect at the single eye. It requires no effort. In fact, any effort we make, any thoughts we have to will ourselves to withdraw, will only interfere with the process, for it means our thinking is activated. We should just go on repeating the Names and gazing.

There are vistas and vistas of sights inside. As the sensory currents withdraw, we forget our body. When we are fully collected at the eye-focus, we become more absorbed in the field lying in front of us. We will begin to see some flashes of light, or lights of various colors. We should continue to gaze with full attention into the middle of whatever is lying in front of us. Look intently and penetrate deeply to find out what is there. Our job is to look lovingly and penetratingly into whatever is in front of us and not to worry about anything else in the body. We should be totally focused on what is before us. Then as we concentrate more and more, these lights will stabilize and we may see red, white, green, blue, violet, purple, yellow, orange, or golden light, or flashes of light. Whatever we see, we should concentrate in the middle of it.

As we meditate more, as our attention is more focused and we progress, we will be able to see inner vistas. We may see inner stars, moon, and sun. As we gaze attentively into the middle of whatever we see, the power of God will guide us beyond the physical into the higher planes.

The second practice of meditation is listening to the inner Sound. We concentrate our attention at the seat of the soul and listen to the inner Sound Current. This Sound is the power of God, the holy Word, or *Naam*, which brought all creation into being. The soul is of the same essence as of God and the Sound Current. Thus, when it hears the divine Melody it is magnetized to it. The soul can then travel on the Sound Current through the higher regions.

❧

## Step 6: The Journey into Higher Regions

As we become more absorbed in the inner Light and Sound that we see and hear in our meditations, we transcend the physical plane and enter the astral region. The physical world which is made predominantly of matter is left behind, and we find a realm of greater consciousness.

Here we travel in a covering known as the astral body. This is an ethereal body. The astral region is full of beauty and wonderful Light and Sound.

When we transcend the astral region, we enter the causal region. This is a region which is still more ethereal. It consists of equal parts of matter and consciousness. In this region, we shed our astral body and we travel in our causal body.

Going still further, we enter the supracausal region. Each region has greater and greater Light and higher and higher Celestial Sounds and bliss. The supracausal region has more of consciousness and only a small amount of illusion. In the supracausal region, the causal body is left behind and our soul is covered only by a thin layer. At this stage we recognize ourselves as soul. We find the soul is as bright as twelve outer suns. It is a stage where we have the realization of "Sohang," or "I am That," or "Aham Brahm Asmi." We realize that we are of the same essence as that of the Creator. Ultimately, we reach the region from where the power of God emanated, the spiritual region known as Sach Khand, Maqam-i-Haq, or True Realm. This is the purely spiritual region of all Light and all bliss in which all coverings around the soul are shed. There is not even a speck of matter in this region. Here our soul merges in the ocean of all-consciousness, the Oversoul, the Source from where it came. The drop of water merges with the Ocean and becomes the Ocean. A ray of light merges with the Sun and becomes the Sun.

At each stage of the journey we experience greater and greater waves of spiritual bliss which permeate our soul. One by one, the layers covering our soul are peeled off until we return to our pristine state. At each region we think we have reached the highest state of rapture, only to find that the next stage fills us with greater ecstasy. The ultimate bliss is when our soul merges back into God, its Creator. This is the state we all need to achieve for us to realize eternal peace and happiness. This merger of our soul with the Creator brings joy and happiness which lasts with us forever. Through attaining these higher inner stages of bliss, we carry with us a divine gift that helps us through our problems in life. We can tap into this source of divinity whenever we want. The bliss and happiness we experience in meditation stays with us even after we come out of meditation. It is a wellspring of love and peace that we can tap into any time we wish. The experience is so powerful and deeply fulfilling that it helps us to transcend the pains and sorrows of life. No matter what happens to us in life, we have a fountain of nectar within us from which we can drink at any time. This is the gift we can achieve through meditation.

## E X E R C I S E

Reread the chapter to understand the meditation technique. Find a quiet, comfortable place and practice the meditation. Begin with fifteen minutes and, over time, increase to thirty minutes a day. As you become more proficient, extend the meditation time to an hour or two. Keep a journal of what you experience.

# True Happiness Awaits Us Within

---

*H*istory tells us about the great Prince Siddhartha, whom we know today as Buddha, the Enlightened One. He had everything one could desire in life: he was a prince, lived in a royal palace, had great wealth, and a beautiful wife and child. His father, trying to prevent a prophecy that stated his son would turn from the kingship towards a spiritual life, kept him sheltered in the palace, so that he would eventually become the king. But one day, Prince Siddhartha managed to venture outside the protective palace walls. He was shocked by what he saw. His father had kept him from the knowledge that people get sick, grow old, and die. His trip through the kingdom revealed to him the horrors of life. For the first time he saw people suffering from illness and old age, and then eventually dying. He saw then that all life is suffering and that all worldly desires lead to pain and unhappiness.

This revelation started him on a search for a peace and happiness which is not transitory, but eternal.

**⟋**

## Searching for Happiness in the World

All of us today are searching for peace and happiness. This quest is universal. After all, no one aspires to be unhappy! People try to find joy in numerous ways. Some search for it in wealth and possessions. Others try to find it in name and fame. Some look for it in worldly relationships. Many pursue amusements such as going to the movies, listening to music, attending cultural performances, watching television, and engaging in sensual enjoyments. There are those who enjoy participating in or watching sports. Then there are people who seek excitement through drugs and alcohol.

If we analyze all these pursuits, we find that they do not bring the happiness they have promised. We may derive happiness from them for some time, but the loss of any of our possessions or relations brings untold pain and suffering. If our car is damaged, we bemoan our fate. If our house is destroyed by fire, we feel as if we have lost everything important in life. If we are millionaires and suddenly become bankrupt, we become so dejected we even contemplate suicide. If we become ill and cannot do what we normally do, we are frustrated and discontented. If we lose our jobs, depression sets in. And if one of our loved ones passes away, we are drowned in grief. The happiness we had during the time we had our money, belongings, and near and dear ones turns into deep misery from their loss. At some point in life, we discover that happiness in the outer world is a transitory illusion. Everything in this world must perish.

Ultimately, we too must face our physical end and must leave behind all that we cherished.

This continual pursuit of outer happiness is beset with numerous setbacks. Even the means we use to reach our ends create much torture and suffering. Whenever we shoot for any goal, the five players of anger, lust, greed, attachment, and ego try to block us. These five passions play their part in tainting our joys with numerous sorrows. For example, if we are trying to attain a goal, whether it is buying a house or rising to the top of our company, we are plagued with various difficulties due to these five passions. Anger overcomes us when anyone gets in the way of our achieving our end. We become annoyed and angry with anyone who puts obstacles in our way or who does not cooperate with us in helping us have what we want. Lust is expressed as an intense desire to have what we want. It sometimes even takes over our reasoning ability. We become driven to achieve our goal even at the expense of other factors. Greed also rears its ugly head. If we have enough money for a moderate car, we become greedy and want to make a more extravagant purchase, even if we cannot afford it. We start sacrificing the money we saved for our child's education to pay for it. We become so obsessed with obtaining money to pay for our greedy wants that some even resort to dishonest means of getting the money. Next, attachment overtakes us. We give the desired object our top priority. If it is a possession, we put all our attention into spending money for it, even at the cost of our other needs in life. If we are attached to a piece of furniture, we become fanatical, and even if our small child puts a scratch in it, we are prepared to hurt the youth's delicate feelings to protect the lifeless unfeeling object's beauty. Finally, ego enters into the picture. We become so proud of our possessions. We boast about our belongings to all within earshot. We feel we have achieved a great accomplishment by their purchase. We look down upon others and criticize those who own more modest possessions. By attaining our goals such as buying a house, a boat, an airplane, or any other item, have we really found happiness? In the process we may have wrecked our relations with our family, have been tormented by obstacles that might have come in the way, and have sacrificed our ethical principles.

It is the same fate even in our worldly relationships. When we are young adults we may desire a companion to marry. Once we set our mind on someone, we become angry at anyone who stands in the way of our being with that person. We build up an image of a perfect relationship, and we may even get angry at the one we love if he or she does not live up to our expectations. We may be troubled with lust and greed in our relationship with our loved one. Then we develop an attachment which may be so strong that we become possessive and jealous if the loved one does not give us his or her total attention every moment of our lives. Ego causes power struggles in a relationship. These five passions result in arguments and fights, and over time the relationship may deteriorate. These are the problems we find within any relationship between two people. What started out as attraction and deep love may degenerate over the years due to anger, lust, greed, attachment, and ego. Thus, the promise of marital bliss may not withstand the negative forces of the world.

Having attained the object of our desire, we are constantly on guard to protect it. If we seek happiness through amassing wealth, that is not without fluctuations. Stock markets go up and down. The economy moves from inflation to recession to depression. Sometimes we obtain a good job and sometimes we are laid off or fired. Possessions are subject to theft or loss through fires, hurricanes, floods, or volcanos. The elements of fire, air, water, or earth may claim our possessions. And if such a catastrophe befalls us, we suffer the loss of the object as if a part of ourselves was destroyed. We may find delight in our relationships, but sooner or later we must experience their inevitable loss through death. Thus, the very object or person that should have given us happiness, brings us pain upon its, or his or her, loss.

This is the way of the world. Looking at the realities of life, we begin to wonder if there is any hope for finding real happiness in the world! If it exists, then how can we find it?

## How to Find Lasting Happiness

First, we need to analyze what happiness is. It can be defined as a state of joy, of peace, and of love. Others look at it as an absence of sorrow, pain, and suffering. If we look at the many ways people try to attain happiness, we realize that everything in life that gives us joy has potential suffering in it. When worldly joys are removed, we undergo pain and torment.

Throughout the ages, the great teachers, sages, saints, and philosophers of the world have been telling us that true happiness does exist. But it does not lie in anything in this world. It can only be found within. If we seek it in the world without, we will be continually disappointed. If we look for perfection in this world, we will not find it. Every diamond has a defect, every beauty a blemish. This is the reason that we find people who do attain the object of their desires move on to new desires. We buy one object or gadget and soon want another. In many countries, people even move from one marriage to another once, twice, thrice, and maybe more. We move from one activity to another thinking it will bring us the fulfillment we crave. As long as we are intrigued with the flashy jewels of the outer world, we will continue in this wheel of disappointment. We have forgotten that the true jewel awaits us inside. True happiness does not lie outside; true happiness lies within.

There is only one source of happiness that is lasting, that cannot be destroyed by wind, fire, water, or earth. It cannot be taken from us either in this lifetime or at the time of death. The only permanent happiness is God. Some mystics of the East refer to God as *sat-chit-ananda*. These words translate respectively as truth, consciousness, and bliss. Most of us would correlate God with eternal truth. And we would also think of the divine Creator as being all-conscious, all-knowing, and omnipotent. But in the West, we seldom think of Him as divine bliss. Yet mystics of all religions who describe their experiences of God touch upon this very aspect. More than their experience of divine wisdom, they are consumed with the transcendental ecstasy they experience when their soul merges in the

Creator. In Christianity, we find that the writings of St. Teresa of Avila and St. John of the Cross overflow with references to rapture and divine ecstasy. Muslim and Sufi mystics repeatedly express in their poetry the bliss of union of the soul with God. This experience of ineffable happiness is not confined only to the saints and mystics of the past. What they tasted, we can also savor. The secret is to find the sweetness within ourselves.

As long as we seek happiness in the world, we will be disappointed, for all matter is subject to decay and destruction. Only God is lasting. All the scriptures tell us that God is within us. The question before us is how to find Him.

Saints and mystics have been able to realize God within themselves, and have shared their knowledge with humanity. They describe to us what God is and how He can be contacted. They tell us that God is an ocean of all Light, all love, and all consciousness. He is the alpha and omega of all existence. He was neither created nor can He be destroyed. He is all that is.

The soul is a drop of His essence. Thus, the soul's real nature is also *sat-chit-ananda*, "truth, consciousness, and bliss." Each of us is actually a drop of this blissful awareness. It is only when we identify with our real self that we become moving drops of bliss on earth. We are moving about on the desert of the earth becoming more and more parched, looking for the ocean. We need to realize that a reservoir of refreshing waters is lying within us. If we can identify ourselves with our true essence we will begin to live in a sublime state of happiness.

ﻉ
## Ignorance Is Not Bliss

With all this ecstasy inside us, how is it that so many people are unhappy, depressed, and miserable? It is said that ignorance is bliss. But in this case, ignorance is not bliss. We are unaware that our true essence lies hidden deep inside. It is encased by our mind, our body, and the world.

To understand the cause of our ignorance, we can refer to the teachings of enlightened mystics and saints, whose words have been preserved in the various scriptures. They explain that in the beginning the ocean of truth, consciousness, and bliss, which we call God, brought creation into being, and separated parts of Himself, called souls. These souls were sent to inhabit the various regions of creation. These drops carried God's essence. When they enter this physical world, they take on a body and a mind. Because soul is spirit it needs a physical body and mind in which to work and communicate with the physical world. The idea was that the soul would be the controlling force within the mind and body. But unfortunately, the reverse has happened. The soul has become so identified with the body and mind that it has forgotten itself. The mind is a powerful agent and is also a lover of enjoyment. It is easily attracted to the temptations of the outer world. The siren call of the world attracts the senses to beautiful sights, sweet sounds, lovely fragrances, delicious tastes, and enticing sensations. The senses drag the mind into the outer world, and the mind takes the soul along with it to enjoy the worldly attractions. Over time, as the soul is lost in the world's play, it eventually forgets what its own nature is. It is concentrated on the world outside rather than on the truth, consciousness, and bliss which are its true essence.

Children enter the world with a purity and innocence. Looking into their eyes, one finds them full of love and happiness. So much joy radiates from children that we feel pleasure to be around them. But from the moment children are born, they are bombarded with the worldly distractions. Infants are immediately surrounded by toys, hanging mobiles, rattles, and music. They start to explore the small world around them. As children grow, they are educated into the culture in which they live. Their training is predominantly physical and intellectual. Slowly, children lose touch with their purity and natural essence. Like the adults around them, they become enmeshed in the world and forget they are soul. The more we identify ourselves with our body and mind, the more time we spend in pursuits which satisfy our physical and intellectual needs.

As we grow up, we are taught how important our physical and mental development is. We begin to believe that happiness only lies in developing ourselves in these two areas. Life becomes like a rat race in which we try to meet our physical needs for food, clothing, shelter, and comfort, along with sensual enjoyments, possessions, and love. We spend time developing our intellect by receiving a good education which leads to a rewarding career. We engage in hobbies and pastimes that bring enjoyment to our mind. We look for happiness in meeting our emotional needs for love and companionship through our relationships with our family, friends, and loved ones. We may look for a companion in life, and ultimately marry and raise a family. We can search our memories to see if anyone has ever taught us that happiness lies within our own selves. It has been the role of the spiritual adepts, the saints, and mystics to awaken us to the reservoir of bliss-giving nectar that bubbles within us.

❧

## Drinking from the Bliss Within

The way to tap into this pool is simple. It is only a matter of our attention. We can direct our attention wherever we wish. We can place it on our body. We can focus it on our mind. Or we can concentrate our attention on our soul. Unfortunately, since our childhood, we have been trained to focus ourselves on our body and mind. Our senses naturally find it easy to become involved in the activities of the world through our eyes, ears, nose, mouth, and skin. Our parents and teachers have never taught us how to focus on our soul. Had they done so, we would have been proficient by now in tapping into the source of consciousness and bliss within.

Instruction in how to place our attention on our soul is the domain of spiritual teachers. From an adept we can learn the simple process so we can experience the pure bliss of our true nature. We call this process concentration, or focusing our attention. But its most popular name is meditation.

Meditation is easy. One of the great spiritual teachers of this century, Sant Kirpal Singh, used to say that it is like closing one drawer and opening another. During the time of meditation, we merely put our thoughts of the world and our problems in one drawer and close it. Then, we open the drawer of meditation and concentrate only on that.

When the meditation is over, we can then open the drawer of our thoughts and worldly problems and deal with them.

Meditation is focusing one's attention at the seat of the soul, located between and behind the two eyebrows. If we can stop putting our attention on our outer eyes and ears for a while and concentrate at the seat of the soul, we will tap into the source of happiness and bliss awaiting us.

Spending two hours concentrating on the eye-focus each day will help our attention withdraw from the body. Generally our sensory currents which give us sensation of this physical world are spread out through the body. As we concentrate at the seat of the soul, the sensory currents start withdrawing from our extremities. They come up from our feet and legs to our trunk. Eventually they are totally concentrated at the seat of the soul. Once at that point, a vista of divine Light and celestial Sound opens up for us. We witness the Light and Sound which emanated from God at the dawn of creation. Like a current, this stream flows out from God through all the regions. It also returns to Him. When our soul comes in contact with this stream, it can travel on it back to the Source.

The journey begins at the third eye. By putting our attention there, the soul begins its voyage to the ultimate source of happiness. This is what meditation is.

God and the soul are eternal. They are all conscious, all bliss, and in a perpetual state of happiness. When we are in that state all our desires and longings for the things of this world dissipate. Our worldly desires become mere trifles when we experience the astounding joy within. At some time in our lives, we experienced some great euphoria, such as when our team wins a football game, or we get a long-awaited raise, or we have any of our dreams fulfilled. For that moment, we are so lost in joy that all other problems suddenly seem like a trifle. We put these former difficulties aside, for we do not want to be distracted from our moment of glory and happiness. This is just a small example to show how tapping into happiness can keep us in permanent bliss so that the problems of the world fade away.

Those who learn to meditate can switch their attention to the source of happiness within even in the midst of sorrow. True, they still undergo the outer pains and sorrows of life, but they do not affect them. They are drinking from the inebriation from within that cushions the pain and takes their attention off their sufferings.

There is nothing magical about meditation. It is something every person, from a child to an elderly person, can learn. Had we learned how to focus our attention within during our youth, it would have become a habit by now. We would be able to do it at will anytime we wanted. But it is never too late to learn this practice. By learning to meditate we can perfect the art of directing our attention to the source of happiness within us. Then we can drink from the eternal pool of happiness anytime we wish. Outer sources of enjoyment may be taken from us, but we have access to an eternal bliss we carry within.

By learning to meditate and enjoying the joy within we have protection from the pains and sorrows of life. We realize that this world is but a passing show. The ecstasy we experience within fills us with happiness and we are able to overcome our problems.

As we meditate and come in contact with the source of all love within, we begin to spread it to others. We will be always in tune with the happiness within and will radiate it to all who come in contact with us. Then we can spread joy wherever we go.

The saints and mystics come to share with humanity the peace and happiness they found. They come to show us the source of inner peace and happiness within us so that life's pains can no longer affect us. They help us to circumvent life's sufferings by bringing us to inner realms that can give us more happiness and tranquility than we can ever dream of. It is my hope and prayer that each of you attains the inner bliss and happiness which is your birthright from God.

## EXERCISE

- In one column, list all the things in life that you believe will bring you happiness.
- In a second column, list all the things that have happened or can happen that can render that happiness impermanent.
- Try to find any area of worldly life that can bring lasting happiness.
- Finally, think about how the source of all happiness is coming from deep within you. Sit in meditation to experience inner happiness inside of you.

# SIX

# The Blissful Garden

*T*hroughout my tours I have visited many large cities, with their concrete and steel structures, their paved roads and sidewalks, and the loud sounds of machines at work. Yet I find that in the midst of this hustle and bustle, people often build for themselves tiny garden refuges to help them gain a touch of serenity and beauty. In Germany, many apartments have window boxes filled with colorful tulips and roses. In New York I am amazed to see park-like gardens sprouting from skyscraper rooftops and terraces. This desire to adorn the mechanistic world with touches of nature is symbolic of our quest to find peace in our strife-torn world.

Despite our technological and scientific advances, the world is still aflame with the fires of war. Daily we hear accounts of suffering and inhumanity. There is hardly a person to be found who has not met with pain, anguish, sadness, and despair.

Sometimes when we look out at a shimmering lake, or gaze at countless stars in the heavens, or watch the pastel colors of the sky at dusk, we may wonder how God, who has made such a beautiful world, can tolerate the tremendous suffering of His creatures. Mystics throughout the ages have pointed out that human beings were created for a high and noble purpose, and the examples of their cruelty that we see in this world are not expressions of their true nature.

As the great spiritual teacher and mystic-poet, Sant Darshan Singh, expressed it in one of his verses:

> This sacred land of God has been trampled with the burden
>    of oppression.
> Life is not a dagger stained with the blood of hatred;
> It is a branch filled with the flowers of love and compassion.

At times, this world seems more like a prison from which there is no escape. But God has not abandoned us. He has given us a key to a secret garden of peace and joy. We can enter that garden whenever we like. We only have to turn to Him within to show us the way.

I would like to discuss how we can achieve happiness and fulfillment in this life by learning to enter the garden of peace within. Kabir, the great Indian mystic, has said:

> There is no need to go to the garden of flowers.
> Within your body is a garden.
> Take your seat upon the thousand-petalled lotus,
> And gaze at the Infinite Beauty.
>          (Verses of Kabir, translated by Rabindranath Tagore)

Mystics of all ages have described worlds upon worlds of undreamt beauty. Rivers of light pour forth from them. Thousands of suns and moons adorn the inner regions. Heavenly music plays enchanting melodies. Every atom is bursting with love and joy. And within us is the One who is the Creator of all – the Lord Himself.

**❧**

## How to Enter the Garden

How can we enter this abode of eternal joy within? As Kabir said in his verse, we need to discover the entrance to the garden of peace within and then take our seat on the thousand-petalled lotus.

All saints and mystics who have entered the inner garden tell us that the way within is through meditation or concentration. Meditation is the art of inverting our attention from the world outside to that within.

At present, our attention is going outward through our various senses. We have the sense of sight, hearing, smell, taste, and touch. Unfortunately, we believe that the physical world is the only reality that exists. But how limited is our vision! Our eyes experience light waves of only certain lengths. Our ears hear sound waves of only certain frequencies. It was only after more sophisticated scientific instruments were developed that we learned there are waves of light and sound beyond the range of human sight and hearing. Now science is showing us that even what we see and hear is not what it appears. Solid matter such as desks, chairs, and walls – when viewed under the most powerful microscopes and analyzed through scientific instruments – is found to be not really solid. Matter itself is made up of subatomic particles, dancing packets of energy, that spin through space. If our senses are not capable of perceiving reality in the physical realm, what about those realms beyond the physical world!

The scriptures refer to eyes and ears that can witness the inner realms. The Bible says: "If thine eye be single thy whole body shall be full of light." Great mystics, saints, prophets, and Masters have had their inner eyes and ears opened, and have not only seen into the beyond, but have journeyed there. They have voyaged through higher spiritual planes and ultimately realized God. Today people of all religions revere these great souls. The best way to pay homage to the ideals for which they lived is to put their teachings into practice. They taught their disciples a practical method of going within. But after the saints and mystics left the world, the inner practical techniques were forgotten and only the outer scriptures, rites, and rituals remained. If we wish to find the inner garden of peace we need to find someone who can help us unlock the gate and enter within. We need the help of a competent spiritual teacher, or Adept, who can teach us how to withdraw our attention from the world without to the world within.

### Thousand-petalled Lotus

Just as we have the doors of the senses which lead to the outer world, there is a door leading within. When we enter that door, we reach the thousand-petalled lotus to which Kabir referred in his verse. It symbolizes the first stage on the inner journey, the region of the thousand-petalled lotus, or *Sahansdal Kanwal*, in the astral plane. This is the first place the soul visits when it rises above body-consciousness. It is reached through the process of meditation on the inner Light and Sound. This divine Light and Sound awaits us at the seat of the soul, between and behind the two eyebrows. If we focus our attention there, taking our seat at the eye-focus, we can begin our spiritual journey. Scriptures and mystics referred to this point as the third or single eye, *ajna chakra*, or *tisra til*. It is at this point we can see the Light of God and hear the celestial Harmony of all harmonies reverberating within. By concentrating our attention at this highest seat of the soul in the body, we begin to see inner Light and hear inner celestial Music.

When we have withdrawn to the eye-focus, we begin to see the Light of God. The inner experience of Light in the early stages may not be so radiant, but as one progresses and rises higher, the Light becomes more and more effulgent. We then become more absorbed within. We cross the inner stars, moon, and sun, until we transcend body-consciousness and enter the spiritual realms within. We enter realms which are indescribable. We experience great ecstasy and bliss as we traverse through the higher regions. We cross the astral, causal, and supracausal planes until we reach our ultimate goal, which is merger in God.

In the second meditation practice, mentioned earlier, we listen to the inner Sound Current while keeping the attention at the eye-focus. The Sound eventually becomes louder and louder and begins to pull the spirit up. This mystic Sound reverberating ceaselessly within us lifts our soul above body-consciousness. At each stage the Celestial Music becomes more and more enrapturing. When the soul hears this divine Melody, it gets magnetized and attracted to it, and the soul soars within. Traveling on that Sound, we travel higher and higher to worlds of unimaginable joy.

The soul's innate quality is love and ecstasy. God is love, and the soul is a spark of that love. We know that lovers are happy when they are united. Similarly, the soul is truly happy when it reunites with God. The soul is a conscious entity and can only gain lasting joy from that which is conscious. To experience this, it must tap within and find the source of all consciousness, God.

### Ecstasy of Love

Even more intoxicating than the beauty of the inner realms is the all-pervading atmosphere of love. These inner regions are dancing with the ecstasy of love. The thrill and happiness we experience when we are in the company of our earthly beloved is but an iota of the ecstasy we experience when we are in the company of our eternal Beloved.

One of the great lady saints was Rabia Basri. She lived in Arabia in the eighth century. She was a great devotee of God and spent much of her time absorbed in meditation. One day, some of her companions came to visit her at her humble abode. Spring had arrived and with it the fragrant flowers were blooming. The companions called to her to come and join them for a day in the beauty of nature. They told her about the gentle breezes that were blowing and of the sweet sounds of the chirping birds. When Rabia refused, they again pressed her to come outdoors. She told them that she preferred to stay indoors and meditate. When they continued imploring her to enjoy the exquisite loveliness of spring, she finally told them, "Of what need have I to see the outer gardens? In my meditations I enjoy the beauty of the gardens within in which I am lost in the love of my eternal Beloved. The bliss and ecstasy within is far greater than the happiness one enjoys in the gardens without."

Many mystics have expressed the joy of entering the garden within and of attaining union with the beloved Lord. Because the experience is beyond the realm of language, they must resort to analogies, allegories, and symbols. These images give us only a hint of the reality that awaits us. Mystics from the Hindu, Sikh, Christian, Jewish, and Sufi traditions have repeatedly spoken of the divine union of the lover and the Beloved. Listening to their descriptions can fill us with a passion and longing to enter the blissful garden within and meet our eternal Beloved.

Meister Eckhart, the German mystic, has said: "O wonder of wonders, when I think of the union the soul has with God! The spring of Divine love flows out of the soul and draws her out of herself into her first Source, which is God alone."

So great is the bliss within that even while we function in the world outside, performing our duties, we are still permeated with the ecstasy of divine union. A Punjabi expression describes this aptly: "Our hands to our work, but our heart to our Beloved."

❧

## Spreading the Seeds of Love

Some have wondered if entering the inner garden of peace is an escapist approach to life. But mysticism is not life-negating. The escapist approach has been termed by Sant

Darshan Singh as "negative mysticism." But the path of the saints and mystics is one he called "positive mysticism." We pursue the inner journey while remaining in the society into which we were born. We continue to perform our obligations to our family, our job, our community, and our society, but we devote time each day for meditation in order to enter the inner blissful garden.

When we enter within and commune with the Lord, we carry back with us the fragrance of the garden of divine love. All who come in contact with us enjoy the sweetness and love that radiates from us. People ask us how they too can experience such love. One by one, the seeds of the garden of love and bliss spread far and wide until love begins to blossom in every heart.

The key to this inner garden is available to everyone, irrespective of one's nationality, color, or religion. It can be enjoyed freely by one and all through meditation.

There is an instructive story about a king who had a large castle. Within his castle were the most magnificent gardens and fountains in all the land. It abounded with the largest and most colorful flowers, neatly trimmed lawns, and walkways leading through rivulets and cascading fountains. The garden was renowned throughout the kingdom, but few had ever actually seen it for themselves. The king invited only a few close friends of his to visit the garden. They found it so enchanting there that they never wanted to leave it. Many citizens yearned for a glimpse of the king's private garden. But if any of them was lucky enough to gain entry, he or she never came out again, choosing instead to live within the castle's confines. One day, a young man from the kingdom was fortunate enough to be invited by the king to visit the garden. He excitedly entered through the door of the garden, but kept careful note of this entranceway. Once inside he was delighted by the beauteous sights and sounds and fragrances that enveloped his every sense. He spent days and days exploring the large garden and, like the others, did not wish ever to leave. But he thought of his friends at home and wished to share this glorious experience with them. So he remembered how he entered the garden and returned to that point. When he found that the gateway out of the garden was locked, he searched for another opening. Finally, by climbing one of the towers, he found an open gateway. He constructed a ladder out of rope and threw it over the wall from the entranceway. He climbed down the ladder, exiting from the king's palace. He then went home to tell all his friends that he had indeed seen the garden of the king and had devised a way for them to visit it, too. One by one, he brought all his friends to the palace and helped them climb the ladder into the inner sanctum. Each person he brought was ecstatic when he or she saw the beauty of the king's garden. In this way, the young man opened up the gates to all who wished to visit. Not content with enjoying the bliss of the garden himself, he wanted to share that boundless ecstasy with everyone.

Saints, mystics, and enlightened souls are like that noble young man. Having entered the garden of bliss, the garden of the Lord within, they are not content to experience that happiness only for themselves. They want all humanity to enjoy that same blessing. They devote their lives to bringing others into the secret garden of the Lord, and their goal is to make that joy available to every soul in creation.

If we enter the blissful garden we will find the Lord awaiting us within. He will fill us with bliss and permeate our being. We will realize that He is with us every moment. He is in us. He is dancing in our eyes. He is embracing our heart. His fragrance flows through every pore. He is the breath of every breath we take. His Music enchants our very soul.

Rumi has described the experience thus:

*With Your sweet soul, this soul of mine,*
*Has mixed as Water does with wine.*
*Who can part the wine and water,*
*Or me and You when we combine.*
*Your love has pierced me through and through.*

The Lord desires to unite with our soul even more than we desire to commune with Him. It is for us to turn our hearts to Him. When our daily responsibilities and duties are done, and the world sleeps, we should run to our eternal Beloved. Turn within and unlock the gate to the inner garden of bliss and peace and meet Him.

A French proverb says: "When a man finds no peace within himself, it is useless to seek it elsewhere." St. Catherine of Genoa, a mystic saint of Italy, has said: "Peace is not found by those who do not meet with God."

Our eternal Beloved is waiting within for us. Rush to Him and embrace Him. We will not only gain peace ourselves, but the whole world will become a garden of bliss.

## EXERCISE

Sit in meditation as explained in the instructions in chapter four. After completing your meditation, note the peace you feel. Whenever you feel troubled by outer distress or disturbance, find a quiet place, close your eyes for a few minutes, and try to meditate to tap into your own garden of peace. Note down any changes you feel about the outer disturbance after sitting in meditation. Note if meditation made the disturbance decrease or vanish.

# SEVEN

# Reducing Stress through Meditation

A man was walking down a road and came across a young man struggling with a long metal coil. He asked him what he was doing and was told that he was trying to undo the coil to make the wire straight. When the observer asked why he was having so much trouble, the young man explained that every time he straightened out one coil, a new one sprang up. When he straightened out another coil, a new one appeared. This predicament is similar to our life. Our day-to-day existence is filled with problems. Every time we solve one problem, a new one springs up. We may be struggling financially, trying to make ends meet. A day finally comes when we get a raise, and then we find our car has broken down, and the extra money has to go for repairs or for new car payments. When we settle that problem, someone in our family may fall ill.

Along with that, we may find that we have a problem in our relationship with one of our co-workers. While that is being straightened out, our roof suddenly begins to leak and we need repairs. After a while we begin to wonder if there will be a time in life when we can be free of problems. We may think we alone have been singled out for misfortune. But if we ask those around us, we find that everyone's life is also filled with difficulties. It seems there is no end to problems.

❧

## Stresses of Modern Life

It is no wonder that we find people undergoing tremendous stresses and strains. The pressures of life are so great that they begin to affect us physically and mentally. We find that people undergo anxiety, fear, depression, and phobias. Offices of psychiatrists, psychologists, and therapists are filled with normal, everyday people who cannot cope with life's struggles. They are unable to deal with their problems. They live in fear of economic disaster. They are trying to handle broken marriages and broken homes. Others have anxiety about the loneliness that may come with the loss of a loved one. Some are so disappointed in life they see no hope for the future.

Stresses and tensions do not just affect our mind. Research has shown a connection between our mind and our body. Our mental state can cause stress-related illnesses. Studies have shown that when we are angry or emotionally upset, hormones are released in our body that prepare us for "fight or flight." Since the norms in our society dictate that we deal with problems calmly and rationally, we tend not to "fight or take flight," but to face the situation, keeping our feelings bottled up inside. The result is that the hormones act on our physical body, causing stress-related diseases such as high blood-pressure, heart disease, breathing problems, digestive disorders, headaches, muscle pain, skin rashes, and other related problems. The solution is not necessarily to let out our anger in the form of fighting back or running away, for those reactions can create still more problems for us in our relationships. We need to find some acceptable way to prevent the mental, emotional, and physical effects of stress which are making us ill.

❧

## Meditation: An Antidote to Stress

In the last few years people have turned to meditation as a solution to the emotional and mental strains of life. Meditation has numerous benefits for our physical and mental well-being. It is safe, effective, and does not cost anything. Once we learn how to meditate, we carry within us a ready remedy which we can use at any time and place.

The meditation process helps us on two levels. First, it helps us by bringing about physical relaxation. Second, it puts us in a state where we are absorbed in an enjoyable, blissful experience, and we become oblivious to the problems of the outer world.

How does meditation work? In meditation we select a pose in which we can remain calm and quiet. The process of meditation helps our attention focus on a point between and behind the two eyebrows, known as the single eye or the tenth door. In this way, we withdraw our attention from our outer body. The body then becomes as relaxed as it is in sleep.

Studies show that in meditation, brain waves function at a frequency of 4–10hz. During these states there is a sensation of peace and total relaxation. But this measurement only reflects relaxation at the level of the mind and body. Through meditation on the inner Light and Sound we receive an added bonus. It puts us in contact with a current of Light and Sound, radiant energy coming from states beyond this physical world. It is a powerful current of divine love, consciousness, and bliss. It is a purely spiritual experience beyond the realm of measurement. This current is within each person and can be contacted at the third or single eye. It provides us with much more than physical relaxation. It bathes us in an intoxication stronger and more lasting than any external intoxication in this world. Our entire being, body, mind, and soul, experiences waves of ecstasy permeating through every part of us.

This experience arises from our innermost self, our soul, coming in contact with its own essence in the form of the current of Light and Sound. If we do a comparative study of the great scriptures and mystical writings of the world, we find they say that the creative power that brought all the universes and all forms of life into being manifested itself as a current of Light and Sound. This stream that emanates from the creative Source was the force that brought everything into being. Our soul is a drop of that essence. This creative power, the current which flows from it, and our soul are said to be all-love, all-consciousness, and all-bliss. As we live our daily lives, we are only aware of our body and mind. We are oblivious to our true nature, the soul. In meditation, when the body and mind are stilled, we become aware of our nature as soul. When the soul is withdrawn and collected at the third eye, it is at the contact point with the inner Light and Sound. When the soul meets the current it is magnetized to it. It is like a water droplet resting on a table top. If you run a stream of water across it, the drop will attach itself to the rivulet and merge in it. Similarly, when our soul concentrates at the point where the current begins, at the third eye, it will be drawn to merge in it. We then start to travel on this current. Our soul rises above consciousness of the body and enjoys a journey into the higher realms.

This inner journey has been described by mystics and saints through the ages. Even today, we read accounts of people who have had near-death experiences. They left their body behind and entered a region of Light which enveloped them with a transcendent love, warmth, and knowledge.

In meditation we can practice this process easily and naturally. The experience is so exhilarating that it surpasses any thrill available in this world. It puts us in a state in which we become oblivious to the difficulties of this world. Our problems no longer have the same effect on us because we are in a state of so much enjoyment. They disappear like waves in the sea. We are lifted high above the storm clouds and float in the sunny skies full of radiant inner Light.

❧

## Detachment from Outer Stress

When we return to our physical state of consciousness, we carry the vivid experience of our meditation with us. We still have the problems, but their effect on us is subdued for we are lost in the bliss we carry with us. We become detached from the suffering of life because we are connected with a sheet anchor or lifeline. We become permanently connected to the divine bliss within. With this inner support, we can then face our problems with a clear mind and find solutions. We are able to make more rational decisions because we see life from a higher angle of vision. The stresses of life are reduced. We are filled with a state of intoxication which has the effect of calming the mind. This in turn relaxes the body. Thus, our chances of developing stress-related illnesses decrease.

### A Special Private Retreat

Learning to meditate on the Light and Sound is like having a special retreat, a special place, where we can find relief from the problems of life. We can meditate at any time of day. We can begin our day with meditation when we wake up to put us in a state of calm for the rest of the day. If we travel to work by bus or train, or we are driven by someone else in a car pool, we can meditate on the way. At work we can meditate during our break or our lunch hour to give us a recharging and to deal with our work situation in a calm manner. If we work at home, we can snatch away time for meditation. If we work away from home, when we return after a hectic day, we can unwind and wipe away the tensions of the day by spending time in meditation. Many like to meditate at night before going to sleep because it is a calm, quiet time with fewer distractions and disturbances. Others like to begin their day with meditation so that they have a protective bubble of calm to help them face the day's difficulties.

By reducing stress we also have a positive effect on those around us. If we are in a state of bliss from our meditation, we take life more calmly. We do not react to others as much. We are better able to listen to their words in a more detached, even manner. Thus, we become more peaceful and nonviolent.

There is a beautiful story from the Indian tradition. There was once a princess named Laila who was always absorbed in the love and remembrance of her earthly beloved, Majnu. Once she was going to the mosque to pray. She was so lost in her thoughts of Majnu that she did not notice that she stepped on the prayer mat of a holy man. As soon as she had stepped on the mat, the holy man jumped up and began scolding her for her sacrilegious act. She was startled out of her reverie by this commotion. He said, "How could you have committed such a disrespectful act, walking on the prayer mat while I was praying?" She was apologetic and said, "I am sorry, but I was so lost in the thoughts of my earthly beloved that I did not notice where I was going." But then, with great wisdom, she remarked, "I just wonder, O holy one, that if I could be so lost in my worldly beloved that I did not notice where I was walking, how could you say you were lost in prayer to the divine Beloved, God, lost in remembrance of God, and yet you could still notice me walking on your mat? If you were truly lost, you would not have noticed me at all."

This describes the condition we reach in meditation. Our problems will still be there, but we become so absorbed in the bliss and intoxication within that we do not notice the troubles and disappointments in life. Our thoughts, feelings, and emotions are not upset or unbalanced by life's stresses and strains. We are able to handle them in a calm, detached, even manner.

As one of the great saints of the age, Sant Darshan Singh, put it in one of his verses:

> *Teach me the art of life*
> *Which makes one a stranger to the woes of the world, O*
> *Cupbearer.*

Through meditation we can learn the art of life which can help us overcome life's stresses and strains. We can discover the way to relaxation and tranquility.

# EXERCISE

Be aware of times when your body and mind are experiencing stress. Observe for a few days how you react physically, emotionally, and mentally to stress.

After several days of this observation, catch yourself as you start to become full of stress. Find a way to close your eyes and relax and meditate. If you are on the job, try to remove yourself to your own work area to be quiet and alone for a few minutes to sit in meditation. If at home, spend a longer time meditating.

Observe how meditation relieves stress. Get into the habit of meditation as a remedy for stress.

# Meditation and Near-Death Experiences

*A* new field of research which has opened up in the last quarter of the century is called "near-death experiences" or NDEs. Doctors and scientists are researching the experiences of people who undergo clinical death and are brought back to life through the wonders of modern medicine. This study gained popularity when Dr. Raymond Moody, Jr. published his book, *Life After Life*, in 1976. In this book he recounted the near-death experiences of people from different walks of life.

ॐ

## What is an NDE?

A 1982 Gallup poll showed that eight million people had near-death experiences or NDEs. When we analyze their experiences we find them to be similar. Their experiences describe regions they enter which are different from the physical world. A typical NDE begins with a person who has some accident or medical emergency in which their body undergoes clinical death. They suddenly find themselves floating above their body watching the doctors and nurses work on them. Shortly thereafter, the people go through a tunnel in which they emerge in a world of Light. The Light is very bright and is unlike any seen in this physical world. Even though it is bright, it is not hot or scorching. The people having the NDEs notice that their hands are also made of Light. Then a radiant divine Being comes forward and engulfs these people with a love, warmth, and caring never experienced before on earth. The Light brings them peace and happiness.

During this time there may be a life review in which all of a person's actions pass before his or her eyes. It is like a three-dimensional viewing in which he or she is also a part of the scene. One not only feels one's own feelings in the different situations, but also the feelings of others. The Being of Light helps people judge right from wrong and helps them see how they can do better in the future. Some people reported that they were given a choice as to whether they wished to stay in the beyond or continue living in the world. Others were told without being given any choice that they must return to the world. Most of the people said that they did not want to come back from that region. Since it was not their time to leave the body for good, they were suddenly sucked back into the body. They then found themselves back in the hospital room or the place in which their body was lying. Many of them could describe seeing the operation that was performed or what the doctors and nurses did and said during the time they were clinically dead. It was difficult for the people in the medical profession to understand how people who were declared dead could see and hear from a vantage point outside their body.

These experiences of seeing radiant Light at the border of this physical world and that of the beyond may sound quite phenomenal. But many of those who have spent their lives in meditation have often experienced what lies beyond this world. Before the 1970s, it was rare to hear of people who received glimpses beyond death's door. People may have had them but few reported them to others. It was after Dr. Raymond Moody, Jr. published his research about people who had near-death experiences that more people came forward to share their experiences. While there are variations in the events of any given near-death experience, one element is common to all, and that is experiencing inner Light.

Some people have NDEs as a result of an accident. There are other people who have an experience of the worlds beyond in the period before they die. It gives them a sense of peace to know that there is an afterlife. More and more investigations into this phenomenon have been taking place. These out-of-the-body experiences might be new to the scientific community, but we find references to these experiences in the lives of great saints and mystics who talk about their sojourn in the beyond, their flights into spiritual regions where there is nothing but bliss, love, and beauty. Those who make a comparative study will find that accounts of these experiences of life after death have been described in various scriptures and traditions of different religions. The founders of some of the world's religions and faiths have spoken of their journeys into the beyond. We find references to life beyond, and to the great Light beyond.

In the Bible we read of the entrance into the beyond:

> Enter ye in at the strait gate ... Because strait is the gate, and narrow is the way, which leadeth unto life, and few there be that find it.
>
> (Matthew 7:13–14)

The *Gayatri*, the tenth *mantra* of the sixteenth *sutra* in the third *mandala* of the *Rig Veda*, says:

> Muttering the sacred symbol "Aum" rise above the three
> regions,
> And turn thy attention to the All-absorbing Sun within.
> Accepting its influence be thou absorbed in the Sun,
> And it shall in its own likeness make thee All-luminous.

Guru Nanak in the Jap Ji wrote:

> Sach Khand, or the Realm of Truth, is the seat of the
> Formless One,
> Here He creates all creation, rejoicing in creating.
> Here are many regions, heavenly systems and universes,
> To count which were to count the countless.
> Here, out of the Formless,
> The heavenly plateaux and all else come into form,
> All destined to move according to His Will.
> He who is blessed with this vision, rejoices in its contemplation.
> But, O Nanak, such is its beauty that to try to describe it is
> to attempt the impossible.
>
> (Jap Ji, Stanza XXXVII)

Previously, any study or discussion of the afterlife in main-stream society was limited to the domain of religion. No mention of it was made in schools, in the media, or even in the hospitals. If people had any experiences, they kept quiet for fear of being labeled "mentally ill" or as having had hallucinations. But once doctors and scientists began finding cases of near-death experiences and documenting them, they found it happening to such an overwhelming number of people they could not dismiss the evidence any longer. Personality assessments revealed that the people having these experiences were normal, reliable individuals. The investigations of the doctors showed startling similarities which crossed the boundaries of nationality, religion, and social backgrounds. People who came from different religions and from different countries, who had never heard of near-death experiences, were describing the same incidents. Today, these experiences have been given great attention by the media and have become a popular topic of conversation within medical circles. This has opened up our thinking to new dimensions which occur concurrently with our own physical world.

❧

## Can We See Light Without an NDE?

With this increased interest in near-death experiences comes another study. People are beginning to wonder whether it is possible to reach these realms beyond without having near-death experiences. If these worlds of Light are occurring simultaneously and people are continually entering them through near-fatal accidents, then why can't we enter them at other times?

This question may be new to modern scientists, but it is not new to many in the East, to New Age thinkers, or to those who study yoga and meditation. In fact, having experiences of the beyond is one of the main purposes of meditation. Meditation provides an easy method to rise above the body easily and naturally. Students of this science have been able to have contact with the inner Light. This Light is not there only for those who pass through the gates of death at the end of their life. It is awaiting each one of us to discover it during our life as well.

Just as the inner Light is one of the main features of an NDE, it is also referred to repeatedly by those who rise above the body through meditation. Mystics and saints of various religions provide us with numerous references to the inner Light. Descriptions of divine Light and of heavenly realms are given in the Bible. Christ has said: "If thine eye be single, thy whole body shall be full of Light."

It was in the fifteenth century in India that great saints such as Kabir Sahib and Guru Nanak began teaching the practice of meditation as a science. They taught that the art of rising above the body to experience the beyond was a science that could be practiced by anyone, irrespective of one's religious background. Thus, they taught this method to both Hindus and Muslims alike. Their tradition has been carried on and, since that time, the practice of meditation has been given out as a method that can be followed by people of all religions and nationalities and from all walks of life. Through this method we can enter these spiritual regions and find peace, happiness, and bliss.

In this technique one can see the inner Light naturally, without having to have a near-death incident. It is a process that can be done daily in the comfort of one's own home. Many regularly see the Light within. Absorption in the Light helps them transcend the physical body and begin to explore the beyond. Through meditation one can travel into the beyond, and enjoy the same bliss and love as described by those who had near-death experiences.

All those who have had near-death experiences describe a world of Light. We must remember that these people are just entering the threshold of the spiritual world, and then they are sent back to their bodies to continue in life. But those who meditate can cross beyond the threshold and explore more of those inner regions. The Light which the people describe in the NDEs is merely the beginning. As one makes further explorations, one finds regions of Light even brighter and more ethereal. Here in this world, we could never imagine a light brighter than the sun. Those who have come back from clinical death describe a Light still more brilliant that does not hurt the eyes. Similarly, there are regions of Light yet brighter than those described by people who have had near-death experiences.

**ﻉﺧ**

## Inner Regions

Explorers of the inner realms, such as the great saint Kabir Sahib and Soami Ji Maharaj have described a series of inner regions of varying lights. They also speak of inner celestial Music. As this Light and Sound current flowed out from God it created different planes. There is the purely spiritual region of *Sach Khand*. Then there is the supra-causal plane which contains a predominance of spirit and a thin veil of illusion. Then there is a region in which there are equal parts spirit and matter known as the causal plane. The astral plane contains more matter than the causal plane. And the physical plane on which we live is predominantly matter and less of spirit. Thus the density of matter increased as the current flowed further from God.

Most religions teach that we have a soul within us that survives the death of the physical body. When the body dies, the soul departs. We also recognize that the soul is of ethereal substance and not made of the matter of which our physical body is made. Those who have had near-death experiences describe themselves as having a body of Light, and seeing other people made of Light. This is why the people in this physical world cannot see them as they hover above their hospital bed watching the doctors trying to revive them. Scientists have begun to question whether this body of Light that rises above the world is the soul. Whether they wish to call it the soul or not is immaterial, so to speak. The fact is that this body is of spiritual substance. Mystics and saints speak of the soul as being of the same spiritual essence as God. The current of Light and Sound flowing from God is also of that essence. The mechanics of the meditation process is that of connecting the soul within us with the current of Light and Sound as a method of traveling out of the physical body. When we can bring our attention or soul to the point where it can connect with the current of Light and Sound, it will merge in it and then travel along with it to the higher spiritual realms.

Until this recent explosion of interest in near-death experiences, few had any recognition of themselves as soul. We have identified so heavily with our body and mind, that we have forgotten our true essence. Soul is of the same essence as God. God is all love, joy, and peace, and our true nature is also love, joy, and peace. If we can re-identify ourself with our soul, we will be able to experience this divine Light and love within us. We will also recognize our immortality. Death of the body will no longer hold any fear for us, for we will see during our lifetime what lies beyond.

### ❧

## Visiting Inner Regions through Meditation

Saints and mystics who have realized these truths have been sharing this knowledge with humanity. They teach us the method by which we can come in contact with the Light within us. That method is known as meditation on the Current of Light and Sound. The same divine stream that flows out from God also returns to Him. It is like a royal highway back to the Lord. The entry point to that highway lies within each one of us. Saints are able to connect our soul with that highway so we can begin the journey back to our Creator.

The connection point is between and behind the two eyebrows, called the sixth chakra or the tenth door. The great saints stress the importance of concentrating at this chakra because they know our life span is short. We have only sixty, seventy, or one hundred years to realize God. The saints exhort us to begin our concentration at the highest point in order for us to reach our goal faster. By contacting the inner stream of Light and Sound in meditation, we can travel on the divine Current back to God.

First, we voyage into the astral plane, and we experience a region of beauty, bliss, and Light that surpasses any enjoyment in this physical world. We experience a delight and a happiness that fills our whole being.

As we continue our journey, we enter the causal plane. The bliss and intoxication becomes greater and greater as we pass through each successively higher region. When we transcend the causal plane we reach the supracausal plane and realize we are soul. On the supracausal plane the soul cries out "*Sohang,*" or "I am That." Ultimately, we reach the purely spiritual region of Sach Khand, where all veils of illusion and matter are shed, and we are pure soul, pure Light, pure consciousness. It is here that we merge back in our Lord. The drop of water becomes one with the Ocean of bliss.

This experience of merging back in God is not one of annihilation where we lose our identity. Rather it is one in which we become all-consciousness. We gain all the Light, all the love, all the knowledge, all the bliss that is God.

We all must face physical death, but those who can rise above the physical body know that there is no death. It is merely the shedding of the physical body for a lighter, more ethereal body. It is like removing an outer coat and wearing a thinner jacket underneath. With the knowledge of what lies after this life, we also become a source of strength and comfort to those around us. We can speak with assurance when we share with others the knowledge that death is but a change from one form of existence to another.

❧

## Transformation through the Inner Journey

As we meditate and come in contact with the source of all love within, we begin to radiate that love to others. We have read about the incredible transformation that people who have had near-death experiences have had. Their brief contact with the Being of Light, and reviewing their life, makes them realize instantaneously what is important in life. They realize they cannot take anything with them from this physical world. The only thing that goes with them is their soul, and the record of their thoughts, words, and deeds. They see how important it is to be loving and helpful to others in this world. That is what counts in the other world. They find that the little things in life that created stress and tension do not seem to be important when they realize that this physical world is not reality, but an illusion, and when they realize their real self is not the body, but the soul. Thus, they mend their ways when they return to life. They realize that there is a great purpose to life, and that purpose is to be able to realize our true self and to realize God. They realize the value of loving relationships with others and of being of service to humanity in this world. They start caring for other people and trying to bring joy into the lives of others.

We undergo this same transformation in meditation. Love begins to radiate from us to all humanity. As we come in continuous contact with the Light and love within, that divinity begins to spread out from us to all those we meet. We begin loving all those around us, and others derive great peace and solace from our presence. We start developing love for all creation. We become gentle and loving to all, including the animals and lower species of life. Just as we would never think of injuring anyone in our family, similarly, we become nonviolent and loving to all in the grand family of God. We become the abode of all ethical virtues.

If each of us learned the art of meditation, this world would be filled with people who are peaceful and kind. There would be an end to wars and conflicts. We would each attain inner peace and happiness and help radiate it to all those around us. We would not only have peace within, but we would also have peace without. We could then state as Sant Darshan Singh had said in one of his verses:

> *I have learned to cherish all creation as my own,*
> *Your message of love is the very meaning of my life.*

The saints and mystics come to share the Light, the peace, and happiness they found with all humanity. They come to show us the Light so we can experience more happiness, tranquility, and peace than we can ever dream of. We do not have to wait until death to experience the worlds beyond. We do not even need a near-death experience and all the physical trauma that it brings to find the inner Light. It is waiting within each of us this very moment. Through meditation each one of us can find it.

## EXERCISE

- Keep a file of articles from newspapers and magazines on NDEs. Look for similar characteristics in the experiences of those who have had NDEs.
- Sit in meditation. Keep a journal of any experiences you have which contain elements of NDEs.
- Note any positive transformations you go through as a result of your meditation.

# PART II

# Personal Transformation

# Personal Transformation through Meditation

In laboratories where computers are built there are special rooms where certain parts are put together. The parts are so tiny and sensitive that if even a small piece of dust settles on them the parts could malfunction. In order to prevent particles from tainting the components, the work is done in an isolated, sterilized room. Those working in that room must wear masks over their mouths and gloves on their hands to eliminate any possibility of dirt contaminating the instruments.

In the field of medicine, when someone has an infectious disease, care is taken to see that the germs are not spread to others. There are certain diseases in which the transmission of even the tiniest virus can be deadly. The care we take in protecting our bodies and the care we take in manufacturing scientific instruments remind me of the care we need to take of our soul.

Our real self is the soul. We think of ourselves as the physical body which was born on a certain date in our present lifetime and which will be with us until the day of our physical death. But our real self existed before the date of our birth, and will continue after our physical end. It is important that we take care of our physical body because we need to be fit to function effectively in this world. It is important to develop our mind so that we can do productive and fulfilling work. But the body and mind will only be with us for a life span of maybe sixty, seventy, or a hundred years. What happens to our soul is a question of eternity. It determines our fate for lifetimes and aeons to come. We need to understand how we can identify with and care for the condition of our soul so that we can attain spiritual consciousness.

☙

## The Effect of Thought on Our Meditation

As long as our attention is focused on the world around us, our physical body, and our constant stream of thoughts, we are unable to withdraw our sensory currents to the seat of the soul. In order to be successful in contacting the inner Light and Sound in meditation, we need concentration. If we try to meditate even for a few moments, we will see how our thoughts distract us. We begin remembering what we had done and said and our interactions with others. We start brooding over the past and worrying about the future. The mind keeps us engaged in a constant flow of thoughts and ideas which prevent us from concentrating. Meditation requires stillness and equipoise of mind. Our success in attaining spiritual consciousness depends upon our ability to still our mind during the meditation sitting.

Whatever we think, say, and do in our daily lives will have a great impact upon our state of mind when we meditate. We can just compare our own state of mind after we spent a wonderful and peaceful day with our loved ones as opposed to having a day filled with arguments with our boss at work. When our day is peaceful, it is much easier to still the mind for concentration. But when we are agitated by problems, it takes herculean efforts to forget about them and sit with tranquility and calmness. The key to attaining spiritual consciousness lies in living life in such a way that we maintain calmness and balance of mind at all times. Once we learn this art, we will be able to train our mind to sit in the requisite stillness needed to enter the spiritual realms.

Our soul cannot enter the spiritual realms until it becomes free from all impurities. This is a simple law. If our mind is tainted with negative thoughts, we cannot sit still for meditation. Unless we meditate with full, unswerving concentration we will not be able to withdraw our soul to the point where we can travel on the Light and Sound to higher realms. This is the reason why mystics and saints throughout the ages have stressed the importance of leading an ethical life. Developing the noble virtues restores us to the original state of the soul when it was one with God. That state is pure spirit, pure love, pure consciousness.

☙

## Purifying Our Soul

If we analyze ourself, we find that our soul is encrusted with a layer of impurities caused by countless thoughts, words, and deeds we commit throughout our lives. Enlightened souls have been teaching humanity how to alter negative habits so the soul can attain the state of purity of thought and equanimity to achieve success in the spiritual quest. They themselves have freed themselves from the clutches of mind, matter, and illusion. They know their way through the treacherous seas and can offer us guidance on how we too can safely reach our journey's end.

To reunite with God, our soul needs to be free from all that is not spiritual, all that is not consciousness, all that is not love. The gateway to spiritual realms is open to only those who have purity of their soul. In this world, we need the right qualifications to enter college or to hold a certain job. Similarly, God has certain requirements for souls to reenter His domain. The basic prerequisite is to have cleanliness of the soul, with not even a speck of impurity. With aeons of negative impressions covering us, how can we ever hope to be cleansed?

The time we spend in meditation and in developing the ethical virtues is within the realm of our free choice. If we spend time in meditation, we are protecting our soul from the stains of any new *karmas*, the accumulation of all our thoughts, words and deeds, for which we are held accountable.

It is important that we understand how the pursuit of meditation and ethical living are stepping-stones to God's kingdom.

The process of meditation on the inner Light and Sound helps to purify our soul. In this process, we focus our attention at the third or single eye located between and behind the two eyebrows. We sit in a relaxed and comfortable pose in which we can sit the longest. During this time we withdraw our attention temporarily from the world, our body, and our thoughts. Our mind must be stilled in order to see the inner manifestations of God.

In meditation, we have to deal with the mind, whose job is to keep us tied to the outer world. It will try to produce one thought after another. Mind is a powerful agent that loves to become engrossed in the world's attractions. As long as our soul is identified with the mind it will also be dragged to the worldly temptations. The force of the mind is one of the greatest hindrances on our path back to God. It will keep us accumulating more and more *karma* to our already full storehouse.

There are three kinds of karma that we accumulate. There is *sanchit* or *storehouse karma*. These are karmas that we accumulated in our previous lives. Then there is the *pralabdh* or *fate karma*. This is the portion of our sanchit or storehouse karmas allotted to us for the current life. Finally, there is *kriyaman* or *daily karma*. These are the new karmas that we make in our current life. At the end of our life, the kriyaman karmas form part of our storehouse karma. Looking at these three types of karma, we can see why our storehouse is full and how difficult it is to extricate ourselves from their influence upon us.

The more we come in contact with the inner Light, the more our soul is cleansed of these karmas. It will become purer and purer until it is fit to reenter the spiritual realms of purity.

Many think that good deeds can bring about our return journey to God. Few realize that even good deeds are adding to our storehouse of karmas. Whether we do good deeds or bad ones, we are still performing actions for which we have to receive either a reward or a punishment. Lord

Krishna has said that both good and bad deeds are like chains of gold or of iron that keep us tied to the world. But the time spent in meditation and remembrance of God does not create new karmas or tie us to the world. It is an action which will help speed our voyage back to the Lord.

*❧*

## Transformative Power of Meditation

The Light and Sound is a stream of love. When we meditate, divine love of God touches our soul. It permeates our being and fills us with love and bliss. Contact with this rapturous power transmutes us into itself. As a result we become more loving. We develop a sweetness and kindness that radiates from our very soul.

In this state, we no longer become involved in the vices that blemish our soul. We develop a loving heart, and cannot injure or hurt anyone. We can only speak kind words and perform kind deeds. We become more peaceful and less susceptible to anger. We become sweet, loving, and humble. As Sant Darshan Singh would often say, "When we are lost in the love of our Beloved, where is the time to think of others? Where is the time to engage in gossip and criticism?" By losing our heart and soul in the love of the Creator, our life becomes more spiritual and more sublime.

Daily meditation helps us counteract the negative influences and impressions we receive during our day-to-day life in the world. The pull of the world is very strong and we need all the help we can get to keep us moving towards our goal. Our soul which is of the same essence as God finds bliss in the presence of pure consciousness. Once we taste the divine waters of the inner Sound Current, we want to drink of it more and more. This turns our attention towards the goal of traveling to the heavenly regions. We lose our attraction for outer enjoyments. We are also saved from the negative traits that accompany each outer temptation. When we are not caught up in worldly desires, we have less anger, less greed, less egotism, and less possessiveness. Since our goal is to reach the inner worlds, all the negative habits sparked by worldly attachments slowly begin to fade away.

An indispensable factor for treading the way back to God is to develop ethical virtues. One way of developing ethical virtues is simply to dive into the sea of love and become so absorbed that we have no time or interest to get involved with negative habits and failures. We will become so lost in the love of God that we will not have the time to criticize anyone or get involved in petty disputes. We will have no time to fight over possessions. Instead, we will be interested in uniting our soul with God and spending time in those activities which will speed us towards that goal.

Until we reach that state, we have to consistently weed out our ethical failures one by one, day by day. These are replaced by the positive virtues of nonviolence, truthfulness, purity, humility, selfless service, and the maintenance of a vegetarian diet. We will want to avoid hallucinogenic drugs and alcohol which lessen our consciousness and are a deterrent to our goal of becoming more conscious. As long as we continue to have failures in these categories, we are besmearing our soul with more and more blemishes and more and more karma. At the end of each day, we need to evaluate our thoughts, words, and deeds and become aware of our failures in each category. We then resolve to do better the following day and eliminate these deficiencies.

If we wish to reach God in this lifetime, we should spend daily time in meditation. We cannot undo our long, long past, but we can take charge of our future. We can use our discrimination to make choices which will help our soul reach its eternal goal in this lifetime. The spiritual Adepts have given us a blueprint for our personal transformation. It is up to us to take the first step.

## EXERCISE

Observe yourself for a few days. Note the number of times your calmness and tranquility of mind are disturbed. Keep a record of the kinds of issue that disturb your peacefulness. Is it anger? Is it greed? Ego?

When thoughts arise that disturb your calmness, say to yourself, "This will disturb the peace of mind needed to have a fruitful meditation." Check yourself and see how you can reduce the number of disturbances from day to day.

# The Nonviolent
# Way of Life

*I*f we look through the pages of history we find stories of war and conquest. At some point in time, a nation may be the conqueror, and then a century later they are the conquered. Lands and wealth change hands many a time. Wars have been fought over territory, riches, religion, and political ideology. The causes of each conflict may differ, but they all involve loss of life, and immeasurable pain and suffering.

Periodically, great philosophers or thinkers come along who clearly express how precious and sacred life is. They try to spread the message to their contemporaries that power, possession, and pride are not worth risking even one human life. We have examples of Mahatma Gandhi in the East and Dr. Martin Luther King, Jr. in the West, who preached the gospel of nonviolence. By using nonviolent methods, Gandhi led India to independence and Dr. King helped move America closer to its vision of equal rights for all.

Humanity recognizes the greatness of those souls who control their anger and refrain from violence. Every year someone receives a Nobel peace prize for his or her work. Numerous other awards are given out by religious, civic, and social groups for individual efforts towards peace. If peace is so highly valued in our society, why does it remain so elusive? Is peace possible in this world, and how can we attain it? These issues are critical not only for the future of our planet, but they are crucial for those treading the spiritual path. One of the basic principles of spirituality is nonviolence. To enter God's kingdom we must not injure any living creature either in thought, word, or deed. Our soul must be freed from the impurity of violence in any way, shape, or form.

♥

## Every Life Form Has a Purpose

This entire creation has been made by God. Every living creature whether mammal or insect is part of His handiwork. Although the lives of the tiniest forms of creation seem insignificant to us, there is a definite divine purpose for every form of life.

Each life form is animated by a soul. Every being in creation is traveling on a journey back to God, the source from where it came. In this voyage, souls are moving from one life to another, aspiring to receive the human form. The human body is considered the highest in all creation. It is the only one which has the faculty to rise above this physical world and return to God. We are most fortunate that we have received a human birth. It is our golden opportunity to realize God. If we miss this chance to realize the Lord in this lifetime, who knows when we will receive the human birth again. We will again have to pass through the cycle known as the wheel of transmigration, or the wheel of 8.4 million species of life.

While endowed with the human body we have two responsibilities. One is to our own self. We should take advantage of this priceless gift and utilize our life for knowing our self and realizing God. Second, we should also be of service to God's creation. We need to realize that the souls embodied in the various species are all passing through tremendous suffering. The lower species of life reside in bodies in which their only concern is survival. The purpose of their lives is to eat, protect themselves, and reproduce. They lack the faculty to know themselves and to realize God. We need to have compassion for all forms of life. They have enough suffering already; we do not need to add any more pain.

### ❧

## Spiritual Necessity for Nonviolence

There are several reasons why those following the spiritual path need to cultivate nonviolence. One reason revolves around the law of karma. This law states that for every action there is a reaction. As we sow, we must also reap. Whatever we do is credited or debited to our karmic account. If we cause injury to any living creature, we must pay for that deed in kind. Most people live in ignorance of this law. They harm others without being aware of the consequences. Although there are courts of law by which certain crimes are tried, many crimes seemingly go un-punished. We may think we have escaped punishment, but sooner or later we must pay for our deeds, whether it is in this life or the next. The karmic law is inexorable. Those following the spiritual path refrain from any violent acts. If we want to reduce our karmic debt so that we can return to God, we must develop nonviolence.

Another reason for developing nonviolence is based on the fact that violence to other forms of life is interfering with God's creation. How can we expect God to grant us entry to the spiritual regions if we mistreat His children? We may consider the lower forms of life insignificant. We may think insects are repulsive and reptiles useless. But for some reason known to Him, God created each life form. To Him, all are His children. What is more, the outer form is but a shell or casing for the soul within. And that soul is a part of God. If we can feel so much love for our children, how much more love must God feel who has created the entire universe? Imagine His pain to see His most intelli-gent life forms, His most noble creatures, human beings, injuring His less endowed children? We who are the high-est in all creation should be the most spiritual and noble of His creatures. It is incumbent on us to live up to the high-est ideals for which He created us, and protect and help the lower life forms. It is for this reason that those on the spiritual path advocate a vegetarian diet. God has granted humanity enough growing plants as food. We need not kill animals, birds, and fish for our sustenance. If we wish to reunite our souls with God, we must keep ourselves pure. We must develop love for all creation. We can not say we love God, if we do not love His children.

We should try to extend to all humanity and all creation the same feelings of love that we have for our near and dear ones. We should realize that within each beating heart is a soul, and that soul is no different from ours. All souls are a part of God. All souls are connected by a deep bond. The soul in us is the same soul that is in all other forms of life. We should see that no injury is done to any soul, for when a part is damaged, the entire system is affected.

☙

## How to Develop Nonviolence

Nonviolence has several aspects. It involves noninjury in thought, word, and deed. There are many shades of nonviolence that we do not even think about. We know that we should not kill anyone or hit anyone. We may be able to develop control over ourselves so that we do not physically harm anyone, but we are quite careless when it comes to nonviolence in word and thought. Let us analyze these two habits and find ways of overcoming our failings.

Violence in word can be blatant. We know we should not call anyone names that would hurt their feelings. But how many times a day do we say things that injure someone's feelings to boost our own ego? If we listen to ourselves throughout the day, we will find that when others make a mistake we imply that they are stupid or foolish. When others reply incorrectly we make them feel embarrassed or inferior. When people make mistakes, they feel bad enough already, but we add insult to injury by pointing out their flaw. Most of our violent words result from our trying to boost our own pride and make ourselves look superior. But in the process we hurt so many people's feelings.

Oftentimes we use sarcasm to try to be funny. We try to make ourselves look intelligent and witty, but we do so at the expense of someone else's feelings. Humor is positive and always welcome. But it should not be at the cost of someone else's heart. Humor sometimes pokes fun at situations. But we should not poke fun at people and break their hearts in the process.

Another form of violence in word is prejudice and bigotry. We find people making negative remarks about people of different religions, of different countries, of different skin colors, or of different sexes. It is a grand step for humanity that in the last few decades laws have been passed to promote equal rights. In the last few years even textbooks have been rewritten to avoid comments that may be derogatory to people of various religions or nationalities. It is important that we do not make any comments that may injure a group of people who are different from us.

One of the most common forms of violence in word is fighting among family, friends, spouses, parents, and children. Our psychological training says that it is normal to disagree. It is quite acceptable to have differences of opinions, but it should never get to the level of a fight. There is a basic difference between a disagreement, an argument, and a fight. In a disagreement, two people harbor differing opinions. They express their opinions but accept that each one is entitled to his or her views. In an argument, each one is trying to persuade the other that he or she is right. But in a fight, violence enters and both parties use heated words to get their point across. People end up saying things to injure each other's feelings. In the heat of the moment we say many things that are not true and are unkind. We later regret what we have said, but by that time the injury is already committed. It is said that the tongue is sharper than a sword. A sword wound may heal, but the wound of someone's words breaking our heart is not easily forgotten. We must weigh our words carefully. If we can differ with each other calmly and peacefully, that is acceptable. We should never let our discussions reach the level of a fight. We should keep control over our tongue and try to maintain equanimity and discipline in our discussions with others. If we can do so, we will find that our issues will be resolved lovingly, and we will not injure or be injured in the process.

It is only when we engage in deep introspection that we realize how many times a day we think ill of others. Many of us have the habit of wishing harm to others. We may not actually perform any deed, but we may wish for a person to experience ill fate. Some people wish that some harm would come to others or that they have an accident. Some wish that others would lose their wealth or possessions. Sometimes we hope that someone else will fail at a goal he or she is trying to achieve in the belief that we will have a better chance to achieve it. If we are jealous of others we wish that they have bad luck and that we have good luck. Once we are aware of this habit, we can put a stop to such thoughts when they arise. The cure for this failure is to think of everyone as one big family. We seldom find ourselves wishing bad luck to our close family members such as our spouses, our parents, and our children. If we can extend the love we have for our family to all creation, it will help us in overcoming this negative tendency of wishing harm to others.

The most common form of violence in thought is criticizing others. We do this with our words and with equal vehemence in our thoughts. If we follow our thought patterns throughout the day we find ourselves criticizing everyone we come across. We think about how badly this person executed that job, or how foolish that person acted, or how incompetent another person is. We have mental tirades against many people throughout the day. Our mind has us so caught up in this bad habit, that we even criticize our loved ones. We think ill of them. When something happens that is not to our liking, we think the worst even of those we love the most.

## The Power of Thought

We do not realize how potent thoughts are. There is a memorable story about King Akbar and Birbal. King Akbar had a chief minister named Birbal who was known for his wisdom. Birbal wanted to prove to the king how potent thoughts are. So he told the king that when a particular man approached them, the king should think evil thoughts about him. The king followed Birbal's instructions and had a mental tirade against the approaching man. When the man came nearer, the king asked him, "What did you think when you first saw my face today?" The man replied, "Suddenly I had an intense desire to hit you." There was no reason for the man to think this, but the effect of the king's violent thoughts towards the man were unconsciously perceived by him and he reacted in kind.

We know the effects of our loving thoughts on someone. Children are very sensitive and they can instantly pick up on someone who has loving thoughts towards them. We are also sensitive. When someone has loving thoughts towards us we respond with love as well. Similarly, our negative thoughts send out a vibration which is picked up by the other person. We may think our thoughts are private, but others can sense them. For this reason we must be careful what we think.

Our thoughts can not only injure others, but can ultimately do harm to our own selves. The time we spend thinking ill of others is time in which we are wasting the precious breaths allotted to us. The time spent criticizing others only keeps us from our goal of finding God. First, we cannot concentrate on our meditation if we are thinking ill of others. Second, that thought will rankle and remain with us throughout the day. Third, we are creating actions that must reap fruits. And lastly, we are being unloving to one of God's children. How can He possibly be pleased with us when we think ill of one of His children?

**&**

## Focus on Our Own Spiritual Journey

The passing panorama of life is filled with many people and problems. If we let our mind get caught up in becoming a running commentator on every other person's words and deeds, we are nothing more than a tape recorder replaying every event. Our every breath is precious. If we waste this life, who knows what will become of us in the next? We should worry about our own salvation. We should be concerned with our own spiritual progress. Let others do as they will. Let others say what they wish. We should remain centered and focused on our own spiritual journey to God. We have not been hired by God as critics of everyone else. Let God be the judge of each person. We should be the judge of ourselves.

If we scrutinized ourselves and criticized ourselves with the same intensity that we do so to others, we would find how many failings we have. If we worked on correcting our faults, we would make more progress on our journey Home.

Let us replace all negative thoughts, words, and deeds with nonviolent thoughts. We should look at others' mistakes and failings with compassion. When infants or children make mistakes we do not criticize them. We look upon them compassionately and realize that they must make many mistakes in order to learn. Similarly, others are at various stages of their spiritual journey. If they make mistakes we should look upon them lovingly and with compassion.

If we can cultivate nonviolence in our daily lives we will find that God is pleased with us and sheds more and more of His grace. We will become an abode of peace and tranquility for those around us. We will be helping God by becoming a conscious co-worker in His divine plan. We will be helping him relieve the sufferings of His children. Our progress will be accelerated and all other virtues will be added unto us.

If each of us could attain this cherished goal, this planet would enter a Golden Age in which there would be no wars or conflicts. There would be no more bloodshed and suffering. We would have a world in which there were only peaceful solutions to problems and conflicts. Sant Darshan Singh prayed for such a world, and I hope that in my lifetime and yours we see it become a reality. Let this verse of Sant Darshan Singh find its fulfillment:

> *From dawn to dawn, let us speak of peace and listen to the*
> *message of love,*
> *The shower-laden clouds of Sawan have enveloped the*
> *tavern of time,*
> *O Cupbearer, let the cup of love go 'round and 'round and*
> *'round.*

## E X E R C I S E

Keep a record of your violent thoughts, words, and deeds. Note all expressions of violence that you exhibit in your daily life. Be aware as those violent thoughts, words, and deeds arise. Try to stop yourself from harboring these by spending a few minutes in meditation. Day by day see how you can reduce the number of violent thoughts, words, and deeds until you have zero.

Note your interactions with people. Observe whether you disagree, argue, or fight. If you disagree, try to keep it at a cordial, congenial level without criticism or harsh words that can hurt others.

Practice sending loving thoughts to those who hurt or abuse you. Note the effects.

## ELEVEN

# Living in Truth

mother once came to Mahatma Gandhi and said, "My son eats too much sugar. Can you please tell him to stop?" Gandhi thought for a moment and requested her to return in several days. The woman returned with her son a few days later and again asked Gandhi to advise the child to stop consuming sweets. This time Gandhi told the boy to stop eating sugar. The mother was perplexed and asked incredulously, "If that is all you are going to say to him, why couldn't you tell him that when I first came to you?" Gandhi replied, "Because three days ago I was eating sugar myself and since then I have stopped."

This example illustrates the high ideal of speaking only what we actually practice ourselves. For those treading the spiritual path, truthfulness is one of the ethical virtues we need to inculcate. Let us examine the various aspects of this trait and explore ways in which we can make it an integral part of our lives.

❧

## Shades of Untruth

Failures in truthfulness can be broken down into the categories of falsehood, deceit, hypocrisy, and illegal gain. Some failures under these headings are quite obvious, such as telling a lie or stealing. Other shades of this trait are subtle, and we may not even be aware that we are engaging in certain forms of untruthfulness. Once we understand the ramifications of this category, we will be more aware of our weaknesses and can try to make improvements in ourselves.

First, we must understand how truthfulness affects our spiritual progress. By analyzing each subheading in this virtue we will understand how developing the quality of truthfulness will accelerate our inner journey back to God.

The failure of falsehood deals with lying. People can lie in thought, word, or deed. It basically means they are hiding the truth. There are many motives for lying. A child lies to his or her parents when he or she fears being punished for doing something wrong. An employee lies to the boss when it means preserving one's position or covering up the fact that a certain job has not been done. People lie to their family and friends when they do not want them to know that they have failed, or have fallen into bad times, or are sick but do not want anyone to worry about it. In many cases, the cause for lying is to protect oneself from punishment due to our failings or to preserve an image we wish to project to others. The most common circumstance in which a lie is told is that in which someone has unintentionally done something wrong. They might have made a mistake or have done a job improperly due to lack of ability or carelessness. Then the person feels he or she must cover it up because of fear of the opinion of others.

In the case in which we break a law, our wrongdoing may be a failure committed in another category. But when we cover up something, it enters the domain of falsehood. In most cases we cover up mistakes which were not intentional. We are not able to stand up for who or what we are. If we make a mistake through acting in good faith, we should admit it and not worry excessively about what others think. Many times we break a glass, we lose money, or we forget an appointment. Our error may have been due to forgetfulness or carelessness or even incompetence. Instead of facing up to our error, we fabricate a story to cover up our failing. We may do it to avoid a fight or an argument, or just to make ourselves appear better than we are. We may try to avoid an argument if our mistake caused someone to undergo a hardship but we do not want to take the blame for it. There are also times that someone is overly critical of us or intolerant of us as we are, and since we cannot control the other person's harsh reactions, we try to avoid a confrontation.

Whatever the reason, once we tell a lie we have to worry about making up a second and a third lie to cover up the first. Our mind becomes obsessed with covering our mistake and keeping anyone from finding out. Our mind may become further entangled in this web when we start adding feelings of guilt, shame, or fear. In this condition it is difficult to meditate. Our mind will be filled with agitated thoughts. In this sense, the lie will keep our attention from our spiritual goal.

If our lie is meant to cover up who we really are or to make us look better than we are, that enters the domain of ego. We are trying to make ourselves appear a certain way to those whose opinion we value. Thus, falsehood has entered the realm of deceit and hypocrisy.

Some falsehoods are told to hurt others. We try to falsely accuse or blame others for our own faults or to hurt our rivals. These falsehoods enter the realm of violence. It is actually the motive or intention behind the act that determines the category in which we have failed.

If the lie is to prevent a confrontation, then we need to develop the kind of relationship with others in which we are not afraid to be ourselves, to be who we really are, and to persuade or encourage others to accept us. We need to be strong enough to admit what we have done, despite what others think. If the other person has difficulty accepting us, and we know that we have not done anything to hurt anyone, then it is better to come out with the truth. After all, truthfulness is a virtue. Why should we soil ourselves with telling an untruth just to please someone else or conform to their perception of us? We should be strong enough in our convictions in ourselves and what we are doing and face the world boldly.

When the lie is to make others think something other than the truth, we have entered the realm of deceit. We try to put on a false face. We hide our true colors behind a mask. Deceit means we lack the strength and the courage to stand up for who we are. It means we are more influenced by the opinion of others than by what we think of ourselves. In the case of deceit we only hurt ourselves. We need to have the confidence to be ourselves. We need to accept and face our faults rather than hide them. If we hide them from others, the tendency is to hide them from ourselves as well. By covering up our failures, we will never improve. We need to face our failings in order to weed them out. Until we diagnose our problem, we cannot initiate the cure.

If we hide our disease and never go to the doctor, he or she cannot give us a remedy. Deceiving others is one thing, but deceiving ourselves only keeps us from progressing on the spiritual path. It delays our progress. If we do not recognize the deficits that keep us from achieving the required purity to be admitted to the higher regions, we will stagnate in the same place until we wake up.

When we color ourselves perfect, we have allowed our mind to dupe our soul. Our poor soul goes nowhere and our mind has succeeded in stopping our onward journey. If we can become aware of the mind's deceptive play to deceive us, we can take steps to overcome its tricks.

Another failure in the category of truthfulness is hypocrisy. In hypocrisy, we say one thing, but do another. We do not practice what we preach. Hypocrisy is so rampant in modern society that it has become part of the norm of life. Parents will tell their children not to lie or not to fight with each other. Yet before the eyes of their offspring the parents tell lies and argue and fight with each other. Millions of parents tell their children not to take drugs or to drink alcohol, yet they themselves engage in those negative habits. Children can not comprehend why they cannot do what their parents are doing. Once children see that their parents do not mean what they say, or do not practice what they preach, they lose trust and faith in the adults. Once a child's belief in the parents is shattered, it is difficult to regain. The children start disobeying their parents' words more and more because they see there is no conviction behind them.

We find many cases of hypocrisy in our religious institutions. Each religion preaches love. We are advised to love our neighbor as ourself. We are even taught in some religions to love our enemies. Yet if we read the newspapers, we read of violence committed between members of one religion and those of another. We even find sharp divisions within the individual religious institutions. It must be hard for the followers of any religion to reconcile the vast difference between what is being preached and what is being practiced by their religious heads. Once the followers find hypocrisy in their religious institution, it makes it difficult for them to have full faith in the basic tenets of their teachings.

A serious failing in the area of truthfulness is illegal gain. This encompasses many wrong acts such as theft, cheating, and bribery. Taking what is not rightfully earned by us is a serious crime for which we must pay. We know that there are stiff penalties in our court system for stealing, fraud, and bribery. Even if one does not get caught in this life, one must pay off one's karmas for those deeds. We should be trying to reduce our karma, not increase it.

When Sant Darshan Singh first joined the government service in India, he found that bribery was commonplace. Despite the fact that it was considered acceptable to take a bribe, he refused to do so. When he was sent to Bombay to handle some large contract, he refused a bribe that was offered to him. When his father, Sant Kirpal Singh, learned that his son had maintained his high ethical principles, he was extremely happy, and he wrote a letter to his son saying how pleased he was with him.

If we are following the spiritual path back to God, we need to develop all aspects of truthfulness. If we are to become a pure mirror to reflect God's Light, there must not be any stain or defect in the glass. Our thoughts, words, and deeds should be aboveboard. As Sant Kirpal Singh often said, "Truth is high, but higher than truth is true living."

By following truthfulness we will make progress and be a noble example to others searching for the way back to God.

### ✎

## How to Develop Truthfulness

What are the helping factors that will instill in us the quality of truthfulness? We need to realize that while we may sometimes hide the truth from others, we cannot hide it from God. He is all-knowing, and He is watching us at all times. We may think that we are too insignificant for such an all-powerful and great God to worry about us, but He is aware of every living thing in creation from the tiniest blade of grass to the large mammals that roam the planet. We cannot escape His ever-watchful eye. He is sitting within each living being. Knowing He is always with us inside helps us to realize that no matter what we do, no matter what we say, and no matter what we think, He is aware of it. We may try to hide the truth from others, but He is aware of all our actions.

Truthfulness involves being able to be honest about our failings. We may hide our faults from others, but we should not hide them from ourselves. Trying to ignore our failings or trying to make excuses for our behavior will not help us. No matter what we tell others to save our face, or to make ourselves look better than we are in the eyes of others, this is not going to help our spiritual development. If we want to make ourselves fit to enter the kingdom of God, we have to remove our stains and blemishes. Covering them with make-up does not make us beautiful, for God sees us the way we really are. We need to recognize our failings, admit them to ourselves, and then work on weeding them out.

We may dress up and try to look nice when we visit a doctor, but we know that when we go to him or her the doctor is interested in our blood pressure, our pulse, and our internal organs, and he or she looks beyond our physical appearance. We may look presentable when we go to our school and take exams, but we know that the teacher is interested in our results on the tests. Similarly, God wants to make us fit for entry into His abode. We may try to cover up our faults outwardly, but He is interested in our true spiritual nature. He is looking to help us remove the character traits that keep us from rising above body-consciousness. He is not concerned with our outward show of character. We may act polite and courteous, and we may boast about our achievements, but He looks beyond that. He knows our true condition. He is concerned with helping us correct those flaws that keep us from our spiritual goal.

If we can honestly examine ourselves and criticize ourselves as we criticize others, we will find our faults and correct them. Recognizing our faults is not a time for self-flagellation or to beat up on ourselves. It is not meant for making us brood and worry. It is meant for us to see the faults, make a resolution to change, and start improving. Worrying and brooding and feeling guilty will not help. It will only waste our valuable time and take our attention away from the goal. We should admit freely to ourselves that we have made a mistake, realize that the mistake is part of being human, and then make a plan to change so that we do not repeat the error. We must forgive and forget the actions of others, and we must forgive and forget our own actions once we recognize the mistake and correct it.

The longer we delay being truthful about our mistakes, the longer we delay our own progress. No one is watching us but ourselves and God within us. There is a story that Sant Darshan Singh used to tell which beautifully illustrates this point. Queen Zulaikha had a desire for Joseph, a saintly and noble man. The queen called him to her chambers and as she was the queen he had to go. While talking to her he realized her intentions and was in a quandary as to how to get out of the situation. He protested and said that even if they appeared to be alone, they were not, for all the statues of the gods were there. She ordered that all the statues be covered so they could not see what they were doing. Joseph finally realized a way out of the situation and remarked, "You may cover your gods so they don't see you, but my God is within each of us, and there is no way we can hide from Him. He is all-knowing and all-seeing." Realizing the truth of what he said, she repented for her intentions, and let him go. Similarly, whatever we do, we may hide from others, we may hide from ourselves, but we cannot hide those actions from God. We may present a beautiful face to the world, but God will see our true condition and will not allow us entry to the highest abode until we become spotless. We must be purified to reach His inner kingdom. The sooner we realize this, the better.

So let us resolve to develop the qualities of truthfulness. Let us be honest in all our dealings. Let us rid ourselves of deceit and hypocrisy. Let us earn our livelihood honestly. And let us be true to ourselves. We should honestly recognize our true condition so we can make the necessary improvements. If we can develop truthfulness, we will find our inner progress will take a leap, and we will achieve our goal with greater speed.

### EXERCISE

Observe the number of times each day you are untruthful. Note the various shades of untruth – lies, deceit, hypocrisy, and illegal gain. Also note times you deceive yourself by not recognizing your own failings.

Try to catch yourself and replace untruths with truth. Note its effect on your own peace of mind. Try to reduce the number of times you are untruthful day by day.

# TWELVE

# Divine Love

---

One of the great dilemmas many people have is understanding what love is. It is a question that has been explored since time immemorial. Millions of poems and books have been written about love. Philosophers in every age have tried to explain its very nature.

Most of us use the term "love" to describe the feeling one has in various relationships. We have love between parent and child, between brothers and sisters, and with our relatives. We have love between friends. We have love for one's country. We have love for one's belongings. We even find in some countries people having love for their pets. Most of the time when we think of love we think of love between man and woman. Then, we have love for all humanity, and for one's planet. And, of course, we have love for God.

The experience of love in each human relationship or for even a nonliving things such as one's home or one's possessions differs. But each form of love involves some similar characteristics. In the case of love for something of this world, there is an element of attachment for the object of one's love. We have a great need for that which we love. We have warm feelings of the heart for that which we love. And we have a fear of losing the object of our love. Whether it is one's family, one's friends, one's lover, one's belongings, or one's country, these elements of love are present.

Each of these experiences of love involves a feeling of the heart. We feel happy when we are with those we love. We feel a sense of peace, of calm, of contentment, and of fulfillment with them. We have an inner joy and bliss in their company. We experience a kind of completeness when we are with those we love.

In order to return to God we need to develop universal love. Most of us have love for a small circle of people which includes our family and close friends. But as we progress spiritually, our heart expands and we develop love for our community, our society, our country, and the entire globe. The ultimate state of love is having love for all creation in the cosmos. We know the joy we feel in having love for our family and friends. If we expand that to having that love for all creation, we can imagine how great the love in our heart would be. This sort of love is pure and spiritual. It is the kind of love that God has for creation. Love is divine, love is godly, love is a spiritual quality.

In divine love, there is a spiritual urge for the soul to

merge back into its Creator, the Oversoul. When God split off parts of Himself to create souls and He sent them to the world, there was a pain of separation. The closest analogy we have is the feeling of a parent who sees his or her child growing up and leaving the home to go out into the world on his or her own. There is such a deep bond of love between the parent and the child that, when the child departs, the parent feels a deep tug or pull in the heart. Even though the child moves far away, it is a constant string of attachment and love that the parent feels in his or her heart. This constant love is with the parent day and night. He or she goes on remembering the child, thinking about the child, feeling love for the child. There is also a constant pull which magnetically draws the child back to the parent. The parent feels as if he or she is not complete until the child rushes back to his or her arms. Similarly, God is a parent to all the souls. While they are in the world, passing through life after life, He remembers each one, He loves each one, His attention is on each one. This is not hard to imagine since we know that parents sometimes have more than one child and have love for each of them. God is always waiting for a soul to turn its face to Him and to return to Him. He knows the souls are lost in the world and its many attractions. He longs for them to remember Him and to come Home. This longing is experienced as a pull in our soul. From time to time in life, each soul experiences a kind of melancholy yearning, a kind of feeling that they are missing something deep inside. When this inner pull to return Home becomes strong, we undergo what is referred to as a spiritual awakening.

ﻋﺶ
## The Call of the Voice Within

There are instances in life when a small voice inside us tells us that there is more to life than what we know of in this physical world. It may be triggered by an accident, by a death in the family, by a heavy loss. We suddenly begin to question the meaning of life, who we are, and what happens to us after death. This nagging little voice begins to cry louder and louder. We start having a pull to search for the answers. This is God's tug on our heart to pull us back to Him. The moment He gets an opportunity, the first moment He sees that we have some doubts about the reality and all-encompassing importance of this world and its attractions, He takes advantage of it. He plants the seed in us which will lead us to start our spiritual quest in search of the answers to life's mysteries. His love starts to work within us, and we begin to long to know God. This is a great day for us. We are hearing the small voice of our soul and its desire to know its true Parent.

As we pay more and more attention to this voice crying to go Home, God eventually leads us to a place where someone can put us on the road back to Him. He leads us to a spiritual teacher who tells us of our true nature, that we are soul and a part of God. He then shows us a method whereby we can rise above this physical world and see for ourselves our true heritage as a drop of God. He teaches us how to meditate and invert our attention to the inner worlds. He puts us in contact with the stream of Light and Sound, called *Naam*, which issued forth from God when He created this universe. That same stream flows back to

Him. It is a stream made of the same essence of God, all Light, all Music, all love. When the soul meditates and comes in contact with the stream it feels a fulfillment and enjoyment because it is a part of the same essence as that stream. We begin to feel more satisfaction and happiness from coming in contact with the current of Light and Sound than we feel from any physical enjoyment. This contact is the power of love which will turn our attention Godward. We find that the worldly enjoyments begin to lose their appeal. We do not find the same fulfillment from anything in this world as we do when our soul contacts the Light and Sound in meditation. The soul then wants more and more of that bliss and becomes more absorbed in the inner Light and Sound. It then begins to soar on the current out of the physical world and into the inner regions of beauty beyond. The further the soul travels within, the more and more ecstasy it experiences. The more ecstasy it experiences, the more it wants. As Sant Darshan Singh said in a verse:

> *I thought that when the Cupbearer came he would quench*
> *my thirst,*
> *But alas, he has come and gone and my thirst has been*
> *intensified.*

## ❧
## Divine Union

This attraction for more and more bliss leads the soul higher and higher through the astral, causal, and supra-causal planes, until it reaches the abode of God. There it finally achieves its communion with God. It merges in its source. The two become one. This merger is the greatest bliss any soul can ever experience. We can imagine this union of lover and Beloved, of parent and child; it is love, contentment, and fulfillment. Yet the experience of union of the soul with God is millions of times greater. This bliss awaits each of us. It is a union that exists without physical bodies. It is purely between God and soul. This is spiritual love. This is the highest love possible in creation.

The love a soul experiences when it reunites with God is far above the domain of physical love or lust. Once we taste that spiritual union, physical love holds no attraction for us. The pleasures of the physical body are purely biological and mechanical. It may give some momentary sensation but that involves our muscles, our nervous system, and the interpretation of our brain and senses as a physical sensation of pleasure. It lasts only for a moment. But the love which we experience when the soul merges with God fills our being not only for a moment but for all times. It is like swimming in the ocean where wave after wave engulfs us nonstop. Waves of love touch the deepest recesses of our heart and soul at every moment, bringing with them bliss, fulfillment, and tranquility. It involves no physical touch. It involves no physical union. It exists beyond time and space. It merely is.

This is the kind of love each of us should aspire to. It knows no end. That is why Sant Darshan Singh wrote in a verse:

*Love has only a beginning;*
*It has no end.*

Spiritual love can never end. It knows no death. Even if the physical body may perish, the soul is forever at one with its Creator. Love fills one's being at every moment, whether sleeping or waking, whether sitting or walking.

❧

## Marriage, Companionship, and the Spiritual Journey

Marriage partners on the spiritual path should understand the role love plays in life. If they want to achieve spiritual progress on the journey back to God, they need to help each other. The two partners in life should assist each other on the spiritual journey. Sant Darshan Singh further elaborated upon this point when he quoted Antoine de Saint-Exupéry who said, "Love is not looking into each other's eyes; it is looking together in the same direction." And Sant Darshan Singh would add, "And that direction is God." If both partners look towards the spiritual goal, they will find a greater love for each other than any physical union. They will find that both of them will be filled with God's love. Both of them will enjoy the spiritual bliss of contact with the Naam or Word. As they progress, each of their souls will be moving along the current of Light and Sound until they reach the eternal ocean of love. When both souls are filled with God's love, they will both be swimming in the same ocean. The two will be filled with the same bliss, the same ecstasy, the same union. What greater common experience can two souls enjoy? Then, both partners will become even closer for they both experience the same indescribable delight, the same ineffable bliss. The two will share something with each other the rest of the world knows nothing about. They will have a closeness with each other which is more than any physical union.

## God: The Greatest Lover

Rather than keeping our attention tied to the earth by attraction for physical temptation, we should strive for true love. We think that we will have happiness and bliss from a worldly lover, but God is the greatest lover. In fact, he is the Beloved. Sant Darshan Singh always used to say that when we achieve union with the Beloved, we no longer know who is the Beloved and who is the lover. All mystics and saints throughout the ages have written about the bliss of divine union. Many have described it as the union of Beloved and lover. The love of God is greater than any worldly beloved. God's love is so all-encompassing, so all-embracing, that we lose awareness even of our own self. We become oblivious to time and space, to even our own name. We are lost in such a great bliss that we never want to come out of it. A worldly lover may leave us or hurt us, but the love of God is constant. He will never leave us. He will never abandon us. He will never cause us pain. He has nothing to give us but perpetual love, constant joy, and eternal bliss. He is our lover, our friend, our parent, our everything.

When we are imbued with love of God, we also become one with Him. Then, everyone He loves, we love. Everything He loves, we love. Our heart becomes His heart and we develop love for all creation. When we look at any beings in this universe, we see them with the same eyes through which God looks at them. We feel love for them, for they are also a soul, a part of God. We love them as we do ourselves. We treat all beings as our very own. We see

God's Light in them. We see the form of our Beloved in each of them. That is why Sant Darshan Singh advised:

*Embrace every man as your very own,*
*And shower your love freely wherever you go.*

Spiritual teachers throughout the ages have exemplified this verse, because God's love flowed through their eyes and hearts. They loved each person because they were one with God and they saw that Light in others. When people came in contact with these spiritual teachers, they were coming in contact with God's love. If we can achieve our life's goal of union with God, we too will walk the earth with the same godly love flowing through us. We will bring joy and solace to each person we meet. People will feel a happiness and calmness in our presence. And when they ask us from where we received this special gift, they too will want to have it. If each soul in creation experienced union with God, this world would abound with happiness and joy. We would all go around in a state of bliss. The love on this planet would continue to increase, until God's kingdom would truly be brought to earth.

The more time we spend in meditation, the more we will experience this love. This will draw us further and further to the inner realms until we merge with love itself, God Himself. I pray that each one attains this goal as quickly as possible so all hearts will swim in the sea of divine love for-ever.

# EXERCISE

Think about the types of loving relationships you have in life. Try to see that relationship through the angle of vision of divine love. Try to recognize each person as having the Light of God within. Love that Light within them at the level of soul to soul. Note any changes you find in your relationship when you love others from that angle of vision.

For those who are married, share with each other your spiritual views and goals. Try to find a common point of sharing and make an agreement to help each other on the spiritual journey.

# THIRTEEN

# Harnessing the Ego

*A* holy man once decided to seek out a great saint and learn from him how to attain God-realization. The man discovered where the enlightened being lived, went to his house, and knocked on his door. "Who is there?" asked the saint. The holy man answered, "It is I." No response came from the great saint within the house. The holy man sat down to contemplate why the saint did not open the door for him. After pondering this question for some time, the answer finally came to the holy man. Again, the man knocked on the door. "Who is there?" asked the saint. The man said, "It is thou." The door opened and the saint admitted him.

This story conveys to us the essence of humility. It contains one of the secrets of success on the spiritual path. If we measure all our thoughts, words, and deeds by the touchstone of this anecdote, we will have an unfailing example of how we should lead our lives if we wish to attain God-realization.

It is said by the mystics that God has proclaimed to humanity, "Where you are, I am not. Where you are not, I am." If we wish to find God, we have to enter within ourselves and fill our being with Him. Right now, the condition of humanity is that we believe we are only the mind and the body. We believe our identity to be the physical body into which we were born. We each have a name, we have a religion, and we have a nationality. We also have the mind. When the soul entered the body it was supposed to be in control of the body and mind. But instead of using the body and the mind as tools, the soul has been overpowered by the mind. The mind is a lover of enjoyments and is led by the senses into the world to seek pleasure. The mind has dragged the soul along with it into the world. The result is that the soul has forgotten itself and has become identified with the mind.

Each person thinks that he or she is all-powerful, all-knowing, and endowed with the greatest of qualities. We are filled with ego. Ego keeps us from knowing our true self and knowing God. If we are ever to escape its web, we need to be aware of its devious trap and steer our way out of it.

᭡

## Many Forms of Ego

Ego manifests itself in different forms. We usually refer to ego as pride. We can have pride of knowledge, pride of power, and pride of wealth. Pride means that we think we are responsible for our attainments. We attribute all that we are and all that we have done to our own individual efforts. We think we are superior to others in many ways. If we could have a bird's-eye view of creation we would discover the fallacy of this way of thinking.

Let us begin this analysis at the beginning. No matter what religious background we come from, we all are taught that God is the Creator. It is from Him that the entire universe came into being. It is He who created humanity and all forms of life. Considering this fact alone should be enough for us to realize that we are but small specks in the entire scheme of creation. He is all, and we are but tiny insignificant beings. Yet few of us realize this. If we examine our thoughts, how many times do we think of God as our Creator? How many times do we thank Him for our life? How many times do we realize He is the giver of everything we have? Few people go through their day-to-day lives remembering Him and His gifts. We are so absorbed in this panorama of life, we have forgotten all about God. True, we say mechanical prayers to Him either at our places of worship or before eating. True, we remember Him when we want Him to save us from a calamity or from serious illness. But most of the time we hardly give Him a thought. In modern times, forgetting God has become so serious that some people have even denied His existence. There are people who are atheists, who do not believe God exists. For many years, scientists removed God from their view of the universe because He could not be verified by their scientific instrumentation.

We can see how far our ego can get the better of us. Some scientists propagate theories that the entire universe has either sprung up as some accident or some fluke of nature. There is the dust particle theory that this whole universe came into being from dust particles. In trying to trace humanity's roots, some scientists have even removed God from the picture, as if we sprang from nothingness.

There are some enlightened scientists who have begun to question how such a perfectly designed universe and such a complex, well-planned organism as a human being could come about through chance. There have been great scientists who do believe that only an intelligent Creator could design this universe, nature, and all forms of life, including human beings. Those who delve into the intricacies of nature and are in awe of it have the humility to recognize there is some higher power responsible for this universe. A majority of human beings, though, go through life unaware of the invisible Creator. This results in placing too much importance on the individual self and our personal capabilities and powers.

Pride of knowledge encompasses a wide range of traps laid by the mind. When our soul enters the body, it works in this world through the mind. The tool of the mind is the brain. The brain is a complex organ that receives sense impressions from the world. We are taught from infancy a culture that makes us interpret these impressions in a certain way. If we receive the impression through our eyes that folded hands means hello, then whenever we see someone make that gesture we will interpret it as hello. Yet in some countries, folded hands does not mean hello. It might mean someone is praying. In still other countries, folded hands means someone is begging for something. The gesture is the same; we receive the visual impression in the same way, yet our cultural training teaches us to interpret it as having a particular meaning.

Besides receiving and interpreting impressions, the brain is a vehicle by which we can communicate with the world. It is capable of learning a code of communication known as language. It is through this facility that we can make our thoughts known to others. We can express ourselves through speech, through writing, and through body movements.

There are many involuntary actions controlled by the brain. Our breathing, our heartbeat, and the release of hormones that regulate body functions are performed by the brain. Certain actions of the brain protect the human organism. When we touch a hot object, the nerves send a message to the brain which causes the muscles to withdraw the finger from the heat. When we are in danger, the brain sets in motion the bodily function which releases adrenaline to give us the energy and strength to fight or flee.

Many think that the brain is the seat of thinking. But there is a difference between the mind and the brain. The brain is like a computer which performs many functions. But it is the mind that controls the brain. The mind is a product of the causal plane of creation. This region consists of a mixture of spirit and matter. With the mind in control, many of our decisions and actions in this world are based on meeting the mind's desires and wishes. Because the object of the mind is to keep us enslaved to the world, it controls our thoughts, words, and deeds. The soul, having forgotten itself, goes along with the mind. As we grow up, we learn how to speak and how to act in our given culture.

We go to school and gain knowledge of this physical universe. We are bombarded by sense impressions at every moment. Our brain has the capacity to take in billions of bits of information, store them, and retrieve them, much like a computer chip. It is a flexible instrument that can be used by the mind to put together all its information in new and unique ways. Thus, human beings are inventive and innovative. Words can be combined in billions of ways to create new stories, new books, new ideas, and new inventions. The notes of the musical scale can be combined in billions of ways to create a wide variety of music. There is no end to the creations which the mind can bring into being. The mind can keep us occupied and involved in this world for aeons and aeons without ever tiring or becoming bored. There are always new and exciting inventions or devices that can be created to keep us engaged.

As the mind creates new ideas and new inventions to change and improve the world, it thinks it is the doer. It has totally forgotten that the colors of the palette it uses to paint have been created by God Himself. It forgets that the notes of the scale that it uses to compose songs are of God's own making. It forgets that the wonderful brain it uses to communicate with the world is also a creation of God. We are so full of pride of knowledge, of how much we know, of how creative we are, of how inventive we are, that we have forgotten that the tools we use are inventions of God.

❧

## Pride

Our pride of knowledge has several harmful effects of which we need to be aware. We not only forget God when we think we are the doer and the creator, but we often-times injure others. Pride of knowledge expresses itself as thinking we are better than others. Someone in the grip of this kind of pride will think himself or herself to be always right. We not only think we are right, but often tell others this as well. We think the other person is wrong, incompetent, or stupid. We think our way is the best. The effect of this kind of thinking can range from mere annoyances and petty disputes to wars. How many lives have been lost because one ruler thought his or her way was right and wanted to do away with anyone who thought otherwise? How many wars were fought because the leader of one nation felt his or her ideology better than that of other countries?

Most of the arguments echoing throughout countless homes and offices are based on pride of knowledge. Bosses and employees argue, co-workers argue, parents and children argue, husbands and wives argue. And the contents of most of these arguments are ego battles over who is right or whose way is better. It is through this means that the mind keeps the world embroiled in useless conflict. It is in this way that the soul is kept from knowing itself. If we think of how long each argument takes, we will find how much time in our life is wasted. An argument can take hours and days, and sometimes continues repeating itself over months and years. Thus, the precious time allotted to us in this life to find God passes away. How much better if we could utilize that time to know ourselves and know God! How much better would it be if we could spend that time in meditation where we can enjoy the inner bliss of God's love! How much more useful would it be if we could spend that time doing something to help others!

Pride of knowledge also keeps countless souls from realizing God. We are brought up by our parents to believe in one religion or the other. We never think that we could have just as easily been born into another religion and would have been brought up believing as strongly in some other teachings. Thus, people in each religion become dogmatic about what they were taught in their places of worship. Few people have the discrimination to realize that there could not be a God for each religion. There is one God. Few people take the time and effort to make a comparative study of religions. If they did, they would find out that there are certain truths common to all religions. But instead, each believes his or her religion is the only way.

In every age, enlightened souls come to show humanity that there is one God, and that we are all His children. They come to unite humanity in a common love and brotherhood. They point out that each religion is basically the same and that they are each teaching the same path to God. In each religion, the customs may differ, the language used for the same concepts may vary, but the same basic truths are expressed. When we are caught up in the pride of our own knowledge, we are not prepared to listen to anyone. Thus, instead of finding out the basic truths underlying each religion we close our ears. When the founders of each religion came, they taught a method whereby each of us can realize God. With the passage of time the esoteric or inner side of the religion was lost, and the exoteric or outer side remained. We find ourselves practicing the customs and rites but never finding God. We pride ourselves on the fact that we know the scriptures of our own religion, that we go to the places of worship regularly, and that we observe the outer customs. We think that what we are doing is enough. But when we open our minds and hearts to learn the basics of our religion, to see what the founders actually taught, and to compare the essence of each religion, we will realize there is a practical way to find God.

Even when we go to an enlightened person who can show us the way to find God, pride of knowledge may also stand in the way of our progressing. Oftentimes, our pride prevents us from following the instructions accurately. We judge everything by the touchstone of our intellect. Instead of trying the experiment and accurately practicing the method taught, we alter everything according to what we like and dislike. We take only the portion of the teachings that fits our preconceived ideas. We may practice the teachings only partially and then get only partial results. If we really want to find God, we need to go to a teacher with the openness of mind as students in a college. How far would a college student progress if he or she joined a chemistry class and, instead of learning what the teacher had to say, argued with the teacher and refused to listen, thinking that he or she already knew everything? We at least need to have some experimental faith to try the method. Then, having performed it accurately, the student is in a better position to make a judgement about the method. But when we do not know anything ourselves and we go to a teacher with pride of knowledge, we will not gain anything. We become like an inverted cup. How can any water be poured into a cup that is turned upside down?

We have seen how pride of knowledge can cause dissensions ranging in scope from petty arguments to warfare, how it can keep us so engaged in the world that we do not spend any time in developing our spiritual side, and how it can keep us from finding a method of realizing God. If we are sincerely interested in returning to our Creator, then we need to be aware of this impediment on the way.

There is also pride of power which deters us from our inner journey. Pride of power means that we try to control others. We want to determine the lives and fates of those around us. In the home, we try to run the lives of our family members. We do not allow any room for their individual needs or wants. We go on hurting others by trying to boss them around. In our offices we try to use our power to get what we want and do not consider the others with whom we work. While we may act very polite to our superiors, we act like tyrants to our co-workers and our subordinates. We make arbitrary decisions to show how powerful we are. Sometimes we are insensitive to the needs of those below us. We try to force our views and our ideas on others. We have seen how pride of power has disastrous effects in the world arena. Many a dictator has cruelly and ruthlessly per-secuted and even killed those under his or her dominion. If we wish to return to God, we must overcome the failing of pride of power. We need to do our job efficiently and well, but not injure anyone. We should be kind and courteous and loving to the people with whom we work. We may think we are all-powerful, but we must remember it is God who is really all-powerful. If we wish to have compassion and mercy from Him, we must be compassionate and merciful to others.

Finally, we have pride of wealth. We never think of wealth as a gift from God. When we lose it we blame God, but when we gain it do we ever thank God? And when we have it do we ever think of sharing it with those less fortunate than ourselves?

For those treading the spiritual path, we must be on guard against the failing of pride of wealth. We should be grateful if we have money and many possessions. But we should not turn a deaf ear to those in need. We should utilize some portion of our wealth for service to humanity. We should consider all humanity as one common brotherhood and help those who come to us. We need to treat everyone equally, whether or not they have riches.

Saints and mystics have love for all people, regardless of their social status and position in life. They see the Light of God shining in each person. They set the highest example of love and humility for all who meet them. If great saints and mystics who had merged with God are so humble, how can we be puffed up with ego? Whatever we have is from God. We must do away with this pride and recognize all as God's gifts.

### ❦
## How to Eliminate Pride

We can eliminate the various forms of pride by thinking about God. If we want God to enter our heart, we must eliminate our I-ness and replace it with Thou, with God. Baba Sawan Singh beautifully explained that when we meditate, if we block the door by standing in it, God cannot enter. But if we step aside and await God's entrance, He will come in. He will fill us with His love, Light, and Music. The more we empty ourself of our ego, the more God's grace can enter into us. Ultimately, our entire being will be permeated with God until we become one with Him. This is the secret of humility.

## E X E R C I S E

Observe yourself for a few days and note down instances of ego in yourself. Note the way ego expresses itself as pride. Try to reduce the number of instances of ego by replacing it with humility. Think of all your goodness as being gifts of the Creator and silently thank Him for each of them.

When you find yourself acting egotistically towards others, look at them from the angle of vision of their being another Light of God. Try to find ways to show respect for others and to work out differences from an angle of equality.

# FOURTEEN

# Selflessness

_T_here is a beautiful story from Persia of a man who prayed to God to show him who was the most devoted to the Lord. God appeared and told the man to visit the home of one of His devotees in a certain village. So the man set out to the place where God directed him. When he arrived there, he found the devotee had never taken the pilgrimage to Mecca. "What sort of a devotee is this?" the man wondered. When he asked the reason for his not visiting the holy city, the man told him that he had finally saved enough money to make the trip, but a neighbor approached him, begging for money for his starving family. The devotee gave him the money he had saved, and was not able to make the trip. The visitor then told him, "Your pilgrimage has been accepted. God has told me that you are His greatest devotee. By serving your fellow beings, you are the true devotee and servant of God."

Every religion extols the importance of giving of one's self for the good of others. There are anecdotes from different religions that relate how someone has found favor with the Lord because he or she has helped one in need. Even if a person is not a saint or a holy one, his or her status is raised in the eyes of God due to a noble gesture which leads to the relief of another's suffering.

If we just think about our own response to examples of service that we witness we can get an inkling of why it is such an important quality. We often read accounts in the newspapers or magazines or watch stories on television about people who have taken heroic steps to help others. We are often moved and inspired by reports of those who have risked their lives to save someone else. We honor heroes who have died for their country. We raise to martyrdom those who have tried to help humanity and have lost their lives in the process. Service is one of the greatest acts one can do in this lifetime.

It is rare that the average person has to face the choice of giving up his or her life physically in order to save someone else. But there are numerous opportunities that offer themselves to us daily in which we can help someone else. The sacrifice may be of our time, of our money, of our resources, or of our skills. But there is no dearth of chances to give of ourselves for the good of humanity.

ఴ

## What Selfless Service Is

The first question that arises deals with what selfless service is. True selfless service is an expression of love. We know that the greatest love in this world is a mother's love for a child. This feeling of affection is so great towards the child that the mother will automatically make all kinds of sacrifices to see that the child is comfortable. She will wake up at all hours of the night to feed the child. She will give up many of her own activities to care for the child. The mother will spend her money on the child's needs rather than on her own. Nobody tells the mother to make these sacrifices. It comes spontaneously from her heart. She does not ask for anything in return from the child. She gives out of an innate desire to do so.

True selfless service encompasses helping more than our own physical family – it includes all humanity. It is a high quality to have feelings of love for all people, both those we know and those who are strangers. It is one of the goals of spirituality for humanity to develop the quality of love and service to all. The Sufis say that God made human beings to give love and service to others. If He wanted devotion alone, He had angels. But human beings are the only form of creation that has the godly capacity to love and serve others. To become a complete human being, we need to have this ability.

ఊ§

## Benefits of Selfless Service

Selfless service presents to us a paradox. To truly perform selfless service, one must act without any desire for a reward or recognition. It is given freely, motivated by an innate desire to help another. At the time of giving, one forgets one's own needs and wants, as well as one's comfort and safety, to help someone else. There are even those who give their own lives to save others. Truly selfless people do not expect anything in return for their deeds. The underlying paradox of selfless service lies in the fact that while wanting no reward, selfless service elicits the highest reward – the pleasure of the Lord.

This benefit may seem to be intangible. But for those of us who are interested in our spiritual development, it is the highest gift we can receive in life. One reaps the benefits when one sits in the silence of one's own self and finds the inner door of Light, love and peace open with ease. These treasures flood selfless souls, filling them with an inner joy and fulfillment beyond any we can receive from worldly attainments. Sant Darshan Singh used to say that the benefit one receives by performing selfless service is as great as one receives by putting in an equal amount of time in meditation.

Leading a life of nonviolence, truthfulness, purity of heart, and humility contributes to the equanimity of mind required for fruitful meditation experiences. But selfless service provides the ingredient of grace which helps open the inner gates.

When we help someone, our heart expands. It reaches out to embrace another as a member of the one human family. This act alone opens up our soul. As our love for others flows out, God's love for us can pour in. As this exchange takes place, our soul currents begin to rise up to the point at which we can experience the divine Light within us. Our meditations receive a boost, and our soul, filled with peace and joy, transcends to higher states of consciousness. Thus, it is through selfless service that we speed up our progress towards the attainment of inner peace and ecstasy.

## ❧

# *Physical Service*

There are various ways in which we can offer help to others. We can help others by doing physical, intellectual, and spiritual service or service of the soul. Physical service means that we perform tasks that will help others meet their primary needs of life, which are food, clothing, shelter, and safety. Physical service encompasses all the activities performed to provide for these needs. Mostly, when people engage in tasks to fulfill these requirements, they do so for their livelihood. Thus, we have builders, farmers, tailors, police officers, and others who perform a wide variety of jobs in which they earn a salary to meet people's physical needs. Then, we have people who volunteer their time and effort to serve others physically without any financial remuneration. When people pass through some calamity or natural disaster, they are left homeless, without food, clothing, or medicine. As we help them through these crises, we are performing physical service. The heart is naturally moved when we see the helpless faces of those who have lost everything they owned and are suffering from hunger or illness.

Sant Kirpal Singh was once visiting his uncle in the hospital. While there he saw an old and weak man lying in the next hospital bed. He had no one to care for him. So Sant Kirpal Singh used his own money to purchase some medicine, milk, and fruit for him. When Sant Kirpal Singh's uncle said that he could understand his nephew spending his money on him because he was his uncle, but he could not understand why he was doing so for a stranger, Sant Kirpal Singh beautifully replied, "You are both alike to me. He has as much right on me as you have. In fact, the entire creation has the same right on me." So we should consider all our fellow beings as our brothers and sisters in God and treat everyone with the same love and care. We should find out if our neighbors are ill and try to help them. As Sant Darshan Singh's verse says:

*We are communing with the moon and the stars;*
*But we have not reached the heart of our neighbor.*

≈

## Intellectual Service

People also have intellectual needs. Human beings are naturally curious and have a need to learn. There are many people who fulfill the intellectual needs of society – teachers, professors, writers, and journalists. There are many people who are engaged in one of the arts, whether it be music, poetry, painting, sculpture, or dancing. These creative fields may satisfy people on an intellectual and aesthetic level. Again, there are many people who earn their livelihood by providing these services to others. But there are those who do so without any financial benefit. People volunteer their time and effort to educate others or to make people happy through one of the creative arts. One who provides intellectual service helps people learn a skill or gain knowledge that will be beneficial to them in their lives. There are many opportunities to help people grow intellectually to better themselves and society.

ঌ
## Service of the Soul

There is another area of selfless service which provides for more than humanity's physical and intellectual needs. People also have spiritual needs. There is an inherent need in humanity to know who they are and to find out about God. Throughout recorded history all civilizations have had a system of trying to understand the nature of soul and God. Whether these systems are called religions, philosophies, or beliefs, all societies have tried to find solutions to the mysteries of life and death, the soul, and God. Even in modern times, people belong to one religion or the other, one spiritual path or the other, one faith or the other, and spend time exploring the inner mysteries. Service of the soul is helping seekers satisfy their spiritual quest. Those who have found answers by completing the spiritual journey themselves, such as spiritual teachers, mystics, and adepts, provide a great service by devoting their lives to sharing their divine knowledge with others. They supply answers to satisfy the spiritual quest of humanity. They can teach the theoretical side of spirituality and help others have a practical experience to attain the same goals within. Fulfilling the spiritual yearnings of humanity is not something that can be done by anyone. It is not a job anyone can apply for and receive a salary to perform. It is a highly specialized area in which only those who have reached the highest spiritual attainments in life can perform. This is the service which only the saints, mystics, prophets, *murshids*, and realized souls can perform. But anyone who applies themselves diligently to the spiritual practices can reach the highest goal. As Sant Kirpal Singh used to say, "What one person has done, another person can also do."

❧

## One Person Can Make a Difference

While attaining spiritual development ourselves, we spend time serving humanity so that others can also achieve peace and lasting happiness. We want to share our joy with the whole world. Sant Darshan Singh was a perfect example of one who truly cared for others. His life was one long song of sacrifice to help others physically, intellectually, and spiritually. As he said in a verse:

*Others are concerned with their own pains and afflictions;*
*Only Darshan shares the pain and sorrows of his fellow man.*

He is trying to tell us that even if others are worrying only about themselves, we should open our own hearts and share in the pains and sorrows of others. We may wonder what difference one person can make. But let us look at the global picture. Most people, in their heart of hearts, not only want spiritual progress for themselves, but they pray for peace in the world. Most people wish to see an age in which there is no war, no crime, no violence, and no hunger. We all crave to see the daybreak of the Golden Age. The beauty of the spiritual path is that while attending to our own spiritual progress, we are contributing to the hastening of the Golden Age. Each of us is helping to bring a bit of the kingdom of heaven on earth. This is one of the goals for which all great spiritual adepts work so tirelessly throughout their lives. They pray that the kingdom of heaven comes on earth so that the world will become a paradise of bliss, peace, and love. If each of us radiates God's love and develops positive virtues, we each become one less person who is causing pain and suffering to others on this planet. We also serve as examples for all the people with whom we come in contact. Each person who begins to inculcate spiritual values adds to the number of people who are striving for a peaceful, loving, and kindly way of life. They, in turn, will affect the many people they meet. Gradually, people all over the world will be traveling together on the road to love and peace.

By serving selflessly, we expand our hearts from our own self to our family, to the community, our country, the world, and ultimately the cosmos. Selfless service comes from an understanding that we are all members of one large family of God. True selfless service encompasses helping more than our own physical family; it includes all humanity. It is a noble quality to have feelings of love for all people, both those we know and those who are strangers. It is one of the goals of spirituality to help all humanity develop the quality of love and service to all.

People who have given of themselves have helped improve the quality of life on this planet. Throughout the ages, some have worked tirelessly to cure diseases or to make discoveries and inventions to make people more comfortable and safer. Others have given their lives for the freedom and rights of others. Some have devoted their lives for the spiritual upliftment of others. Each of us in our own sphere can use our God-given talents and our knowledge and skills selflessly to make a contribution to make the world a better place for all life.

## E X E R C I S E

Note opportunities that arise for you to offer selfless service to others physically, intellectually, financially, and spiritually. Note how you respond to these opportunities.

Begin to spend some time daily in selfless service. Find chances to increase time spent in selfless service. Note the effect it has on your life.

# PART III

# Outer Peace

# FIFTEEN

# A World of Unity
# and Peace

---

*I*f we look at any objects in nature or some items made by human hands, we may find there is a beauty, a symmetry, and a wholeness in their form. Whenever any object breaks, it becomes fragmented and disjointed. We feel agitated when something breaks, and we want to either discard it or piece it back together again. When anything we admire is shattered to pieces, the peace of the atmosphere and our peace of mind is disturbed.

We find that we have within us an innate sense of oneness and unity. This does not only extend to objects, but to human relations. We crave for unity in our family, among our friends, within our sports team, and within our community and country. There is peace and contentment when a mother holds her child. There is love and joy when lover and beloved meet. There is a sense of understanding and happiness when two friends sit together. When this one-ness is lacking, there is a sense of disharmony.

❧

## Our Essential Unity

Unity is a condition which underlies God's creation. The peace we feel in unity is a reflection of our true state of existence. It is a state in which there is only one. That original unity is God Himself. Many Judeo-Christian and Hindu scriptures refer to the state before creation came into being. They agree that in the beginning there was only God.

In the *Rig Veda* it is written:

*In the beginning was Prajapati, the Brahman, with whom was the Word and the Word was verily the Supreme Brahman.*

In the Bible it says:

*All things were made by Him; and without Him was not anything made that was made. In Him was life; and the life was the light of man.*

There was no division, no separation, no duality. He was a formless ocean of all consciousness, all bliss, and all Light. There was no caste, no religion, no nationality. It was only when God decided to express Himself and bring creation into being that unity became duality. What was one became many. The above scriptures refer to this initial urge; they describe creation as God expressing Himself into two primal manifestations: Light and Sound.

As part of His divine creative plan, parts of Himself were separated and sent to inhabit these worlds. These small particles of His essence are called souls. They carried with them all the qualities of God: consciousness, bliss, and Light. When they were sent to the various worlds they were environed by outer bodies made of the material of the plane in which they resided. In the purely spiritual realms, they were all spirit. As they descended to regions made of matter, they were covered by layers of that same matter. Thus, on this physical plane, they reside in physical bodies. Over aeons of time, the soul became identified with the body and the region it inhabited. It has, unfortunately, forgotten its true identity as soul.

If we were to look down upon this physical world from a high vantage point, we would find the light of billions of souls shimmering throughout the world. Like a foaming sea, they move about from one life to another, from one form of living thing to another. All the souls, when seen in their true perspective, are the same. They are all a part of God's consciousness; they are all Light, and they all have an innate bliss. But if we look at the condition of our world, we are appalled and shocked by the suffering and pain each form of life is undergoing. We find strife and dissension throughout the world. We find countries at war. Many nations are embroiled in internal conflicts. We see religious groups at odds with each other. Community strife is widespread. Even within families we find discord and disharmony. We find human beings killing various forms of life, including other human beings.

We wonder how there can be so much pain and turmoil caused by people who have within them the same divinity of God. This seeming "fragmentation" of God into so many souls was meant to bring an increase in the Lord's happiness. Just as a couple bear children to increase their mutual love and joy, so did God bring about the creation of so many souls, so many children. Yet the result is far from what was intended. We who are moving packets of bliss and all-consciousness are aware of great pain and torment.

❧

## Rediscovering Our Unity

If we could return to our true state and realize we are soul, we would find lasting peace and ecstasy. If we could tap deeply within ourselves, penetrating beyond the outer form of this physical body and mind, we would find a wellspring of eternal peace and happiness. We would discover the secret of unity underlying this universe.

When we examine our day-to-day life, we may question how it is possible to realize our true self and God. So many years of our life have already passed and we have not gained any such awareness. Like any field of learning, we need to have the proper education, an experienced teacher, and the right technique. Spiritual knowledge of our soul and God is available to each of us. It has been accessible to people in all times. There are many fortunate people who have discovered the unity and peace within themselves. Having found their true selves and the Creator, they are often moved to share their experience with their fellow beings. The bliss they enjoy is so great they want everyone else to experience it as well. These compassionate souls are known by us as saints, mystics, prophets, or spiritual teachers. They want to eliminate the suffering in this world caused by ignorance of our true nature.

They all used a method of inversion to find their true selves. In various scriptures they may refer to this as prayer, contemplation, worship, or meditation. Whatever it is called, the process is the same. We must concentrate our attention within us. When great saints and mystics came to this world, they taught this technique to their disciples. Unfortunately, after they left the world, their original instructions, which were usually passed on by word of mouth secretly to their disciples, were lost. Thus, all we are left with are the outer rites and rituals which we follow at our various churches, temples, and other places of worship. We are fortunate that in modern times we have access to meditation instructions. These instructions are available to humanity at large and hundreds of thousands of people have benefitted from them. Through meditation we can tap into the fount of bliss, Light, and joy within us and return to our original state of unity with God.

### ❧

## Union with God

It is difficult to describe – using the limitations of human language – the absolute ecstasy one experiences when one becomes reunited with God. There is a peace, satisfaction, and harmony which fills us so completely. The soul achieves its ultimate fulfillment and rests eternally in joy and happiness. The only comparison that gives us some concept of what this rapturous state is like is the happiness a parent feels when its child is in its arms, or of the nuptial union of a bride and bridegroom. Even these are pale comparisons of the delight the soul experiences when returned to the lap of God.

A great realization dawns on the soul that attains union with God. It recognizes itself as a soul which has merged with the Oversoul. It begins to see the Light of the soul in all other beings. Its spiritual vision is fully opened and it sees all life as a part of God. It realizes that every soul in creation is a child of God and is its own brother and sister as well. A love wells up in such a soul for all creation. When it looks at another human being, or an animal, or plant, it sees the Light of God shining within it. Just as we have an innate love for our close family members, we begin to love all creation with that same love.

❧

## How to Attain Human Unity

Many noble-hearted souls have been calling for human unity. This trend has gained in momentum over the last few decades. Yet, despite the popular growth in movements for unity, we still find conflict and discord in the world. Speeches and conferences are motivated by high ideals. They inspire the participants to turn their attention to the goal of oneness. But unity comes about only at the personal level, when each one experiences it for one's self. When we merge in God and see the Light of God in every being, we have truly realized unity. It then becomes easy for us to love all, because we see our own self in each being. If we truly wish to achieve human oneness, we must first experience it ourselves.

Just imagine what a beautiful world we would have if every person saw God's Light in every other form of creation! We could then exclaim as Sant Darshan Singh did in one of his exquisite verses:

*I have learned to cherish all creation as my own,*
*Your message of love is the very meaning of my life.*

There would be an atmosphere of peace and tranquility. Gentleness would flow from our lips. Tenderness would exude from our actions. Sweetness would pour from our eyes. All who came within our ambit would feel serenity and joy. If anyone has been lucky enough to have spent some time in the company of great spiritual teachers, he or she would have felt a tremendous love and peace in their company. Any time we go to spiritual adepts with a troubled heart, we feel that our pain has been relieved and our burdens lifted. They speak to us lovingly, they embrace us affectionately, and they care for us from the depths of their heart and soul. The world and its troubles disappear when we are in their presence. We feel as if we are living in moments of eternity. Time stands still, and our difficulties vanish. This is the result of being in the company of someone who has merged with God and who loves all creation as if they were a part of one large family. What they have attained is possible for each of us to attain. Wouldn't it be wonderful if we felt this love and harmony radiating from everyone we met?

The world was meant to be a garden of Eden and a haven of bliss. To attain such a paradise on earth, each of us has to make a contribution. Peace and unity begin within each one of us. We cannot expect others to radiate harmony and oneness if we ourselves are not prepared to see their fruition in our own lives. Each of us must do his or her own small part to bring about the fulfillment of this noble dream. We can attain this condition by the process of meditation that leads to self-knowledge and God-realization.

When we begin to have love for all, a transformation

occurs within us. Our whole behavior towards others changes. We become nonviolent in all our dealings. We begin to have understanding and compassion towards the idiosyncrasies and habits of others. We stop criticizing people in our minds. First, we realize that they are bound by the shrouds of ignorance and illusion of this world. We know that deep within them is the soul, a part of God, and that it is only their mind and their state of spiritual ignorance that causes them to behave the way they do. Second, we are so steeped in God's love and the bliss which permeates us that we do not want to be distracted from that rapturous state by petty thoughts of others. We are so far removed from the trifles that people become involved in that we do not recognize them. Criticizing others in our thoughts only pulls us away from the state of happiness that union with God brings. Since our thoughts will be filled with divine love of God, our words will become sweet and loving. We will not say anything unkind to anyone. People who come within our sphere will find only words of love and kindness. Even if some short word escapes our lips accidentally, we will feel the pain we cause someone else and will immediately apologize and set the relationship right. We will become sensitive to the hearts of others and will wish them no harm. Finally, we will never do anything to physically harm anyone. We will not become violent with anyone. We will even have regard for the life of animals. This is why people who are serious about treading the path Godwards become vegetarian. They do not wish to take the life of any other creature, because they see God's Light shining within all creation.

When this unity is attained, the divisions that separate

human beings from one another will fall away. As Sant Darshan Singh once prayed in a verse:

*Your tipplers are divided by temple and mosque;*
*Remove the barriers that separate them, Cupbearer.*

ﻌﺺ
## Unity in Diversity

Whether we pray in a temple or a mosque, we will all realize that each person, irrespective of the religion into which he or she was born, is praying to one God. We will recognize that God is one, whether he is called God, Allah, Jehovah, Wahiguru, Parmatma, the Oversoul, the creative power of the universe, or any other name. We will see unity in the diversity of life. It will not matter to us whether someone is Hindu or Muslim, Sikh or Jain, Christian or Jewish, Buddhist or Parsi. We will recognize God's Light in each being, whether their outer skin is black, white, or tan. We will know that God resides in every person, whether born in Asia, Africa, Australia, Europe, North America, or South America. We will realize that the same Light of God is in each of them. We will appreciate the differences caused by tradition and cultures, but realize there is a unity in all living beings.

Through meditation, we can transform ourselves into ambassadors of God's love and Light on earth. There are many goals which people work towards in life. But the highest aim to which we can devote ourselves is human unity. The path towards unity begins with each of us. We must first attain our union with God. Then, human unity will become a natural by-product. We will spread the fragrance of unity wherever we go. Others will be inspired by our example and will begin to emulate us. One by one, step by step, all human beings will find that they can attain true happiness and personal fulfillment by merging their souls with God through the process of meditation. In this way, we can bring about peace and unity on our planet. We have already spent much of our lifetime involved in the pursuit of worldly goals and attainments. We can evaluate how much happiness we have attained. We can think about whether we have eliminated suffering, pain, and hardship from our lives. We can look at the condition of the world.

Peace and unity are assured us when we achieve the union of our soul with God. If we feel that this is a goal we would like to accomplish in the remaining years of our life, there is a way to make it a reality. It is my hope and prayer that each person finds inner peace and unity, and can spread it throughout the world. We owe our gratitude to the great spiritual teachers who have given us the tools and technique to reach this goal. Let us take advantage of this golden opportunity, for we will not only be helping our own selves and our loved ones, but we will transform the world into one of peace and unity.

As Sant Darshan Singh prayed in another verse:

*May the bond of brotherhood knit us all together,*
*And may the entire universe be at peace under your*
    *protective wings.*

## EXERCISE

Examine your own attitudes towards human unity. Try to recognize any signs in yourself of prejudice or discrimination towards people of other nations, religions, social classes, or beliefs.

Think of the people or groups for whom you feel prejudice. Recognize that the same Light of God is in them as is in you. Practice recognizing the Light in others whom you meet. Note the effect this new way of thinking has on your life.

# SIXTEEN

# Ecology of the Soul

_W_e have witnessed more scientific and technological advances in the past four decades than in all previous recorded history. Scientists have uncovered many of the laws which govern nature itself. The more they learn about the mysteries of nature, the more they marvel at the perfection of the universe. Many now proclaim that the universe cannot be haphazard, but must be the design of some higher power.

There is a perfect balance in nature. Our world, our environment, and nature itself form a living, interdependent system. Seen from the proper perspective, there is no division or duality. Life itself appears to be a single unit. It is a living, conscious entity. It was formed by the hands of the Creator and was animated by His life breath.

The perfect balance of nature which has maintained life

on our planet for millions of years is being threatened by the very technology that has transformed the modern world. Every day the media report new threats to the environment. The air we breathe, the water we drink, and the land from which we derive our food are all progressively polluted. The very atmosphere protecting the earth is endangered. The concern for the ecology of our planet is not limited to any one country or part of the world. We face a global problem.

Concern for the ecology has become one of the main preoccupations of the world. If we look into the etymology of the word "ecology" we find that it comes from the Greek language. The Greek word *oikos* means "house" or "dwelling place." The element "logy" means "the study of." So the word originally meant "the study of our house or dwelling place." Today when we think of the study of our dwelling place our thoughts turn to the earth and Mother Nature. We may divide this study into four areas: understanding the cycles of nature, becoming aware of the effects of pollution, learning how to restore nature to its pristine beauty, and putting into practice methods to preserve the purity of nature. We may think of these four areas as: natural cycles, pollution, restoration, and preservation.

There is another way of understanding the word ecology. Saints and mystics refer to our home or dwelling place as the physical body which God Himself has made. The indweller of this house is the soul. The scriptures tell us that we have a responsibility to maintain and preserve the purity and beauty of the soul and its dwelling place. Unfortunately, we have largely ignored our spiritual side and have sacrificed its purity for the sake of the transitory world.

I would like to examine the "ecology of the soul." The same four areas of study apply to the inner and the outer ecology. There are fundamental laws and cycles that apply to the spirit just as to nature. We can gain an awareness of how pollution affects us within as well as how it affects the world around us. We can learn how to restore nature and our own self to their original beauty. And we can put into practice methods to preserve our spiritual purity.

ॐ

## Natural Cycles

All life forms one perfect tapestry. Fundamental laws and cycles underlie existence. The life cycle in nature is an example of perfect interconnectedness. Water from the seas evaporates and turns into water vapor. In this process, impurities and minerals are left behind. The vapor forms into clouds, which are blown across the land. As the clouds meet cool air, the water condenses into water droplets, and these pour down as rain or snow which nourishes life. For countless ages this cycle has brought water from the abundant oceans to the land so that animals and people can have fresh water to drink and green plants can flourish.

With all our advances, we have not devised a technology that can duplicate the method by which green plants convert sunlight, carbon dioxide, and water into food and oxygen. Through this simple process the earth receives a fresh supply of oxygen, necessary for all life, and an inexhaustible store of food is available.

There is a perfect design in nature. Even death helps to bring forth life. When plants and animals die, their decomposed bodies provide essential minerals for crops. After millions of years the decomposed material forms into energy-producing fossil fuels. The ecological system which God created on our earth is so unique that ours is the only habitable planet in our solar system.

Like other natural cycles – such as the water cycle, the plant cycle, and the fossil-fuel cycle – there is also a cycle of the soul. The soul's journey began with the creation of the universes, and it has been in motion ever since.

The scriptures tell us that in the beginning God was all alone. He was an ocean of all blissful consciousness. Then He decided to become many from One. This thought set in motion a vibration, which resulted in two primal manifestations: Light and Sound. All scriptures speak of this Light and Sound by various names. This Word or Naam was the God-into-expression power. It created various planes of existence: the purely spiritual plane of Sach Khand, the supra-causal plane, the causal plane, the astral plane, and the material realms of this physical plane. It created human beings and all other species of life. It is this creative power which keeps the universe running in perfect symmetry and harmony, holding planets in their orbit and the stars in the heavens.

The soul is a spark of that creative principle. It is the enlivening force within us. As long as the soul inhabits the body, the body is alive. At the time of physical death, the soul departs that body for good. When God created the universes, He separated souls from Himself to inhabit the worlds. Thus began the cycle of the soul. For aeons it has been inhabiting the various planes of creation, taking up residence in one life form or another. When life in one body or life form ends, the soul returns to inhabit another. As a plant dies in the winter to regenerate in the spring, so does the soul transmigrate. When one life is over, it begins another, in a new form. Nothing is lost in nature. The soul, being a spark of the immortal God, never dies. It simply moves from one life to another.

God, while separating souls from Himself, has also provided a way for souls to return to Him. This way back to Him is through the current of Naam or Word. But, in the scheme of creation, it has been so ordained that the soul does not remember its past existence until it has achieved spiritual evolution. If we were to recall each previous birth, our present life would be so complicated with memories of former ties, it would be difficult to function within our existing relationships. We would be seeking out our parents, spouses, and children from previous births. Thus, a cloud of forgetfulness covers each soul when it enters a new birth. It has also forgotten its true nature as soul, a drop of God. In its successive births, the soul, in its state of ignorance, identifies with the mind and body. Instead of seeking the way back to its Source, it is attracted to the temptations of the world.

The knowledge of our true self lies buried in the deepest recesses of our innermost soul. Like a diamond buried deep within the earth, or the layers of rich oil lying far below the earth's surface, our most precious treasure, the soul, lies buried beneath layers of mind, matter, and illusion. We need to tap into it during our present life span to uncover our greatest resource.

❧

## Pollution

The next aspect of inner and outer ecology is pollution. Like air and water, the soul has an innate beauty of its own. It is made of the same essence as God. As Sant Kirpal Singh beautifully said, "God is love, the soul being of the same essence as God is love, and the way back to God is also through love."

For millions of years our earth has had clean air and fresh flowing waters. But our exploitation of the planet has sullied these natural resources. We have polluted our air, water, and soil and are destroying the earth's ozone layer, its forests, and its animals. In a similar fashion, our in-satiable appetite for gratifying our senses has polluted the natural purity of the soul.

When soul inhabits a physical body it must work through a physical mind and the sense organs. Many of us think that our seat of intelligence is the brain. But the brain is merely a tool, like a complex computer, through which the soul communicates with and receives impressions from the outer world. The operator behind the machinery of the body and mind is the soul. The soul should have been in control of the mind and body, but the situation has been reversed. The soul is now led by the mind and has been caught up in the sensory impressions of the world.

The sights and sounds, the aromas and tastes, and the intriguing sensations of the world have attracted our atten-tion, which is the outer expression of our soul. As a result our attention has been dragged outward through the nine doors of the body: the two eyes, two ears, two nostrils, the mouth, and two organs below. The mind, being a lover of enjoyment, has pulled our consciousness into the physical world, and we have forgotten our true self.

We pass our life caught up in sensuous and worldly pleasures. We have come to believe that the purpose of our life is to amass worldly and material gifts such as wealth, possessions, relations, name and fame, and power. We forget that none of these can go with us when we die. They are as vaporous as mirages in the desert. We depart from the world as we came in – as soul, devoid of any material belongings.

For many, this realization occurs too late. The worldly desires and sensuous pleasures settle like dust on the pure soul. After aeons of coming and going in the world, our soul has become so covered with the pollution of worldly impressions that we cannot recognize ourselves. But there are some fortunate souls who experience an awakening. They come to realize that there is a spiritual significance to life. An innate desire for immortality moves these souls to solve the mystery of life and death. When the questions of who are we, why are we here, and where do we go arise within us, a spiritual spark is ignited. We cannot rest until we find the answer. A sincere cry issues forth from deep within us, and we pray to the Lord for help and guidance.

ᵃ§

## Restoring the Beauty of the Soul

The third aspect of this subject is restoring the beauty of the soul. The ecologists who work to clean our polluted air and water, and to free those animals trapped in the muck of oil spills, are the environmental heroes and heroines of our times. We also have in our world ecologists of the soul. These beings have realized the pristine beauty of the spirit and are aware of those pollutants that cover it with layers of dirt and filth. They too are working constantly to find those seekers trapped in worldly desires so they can be set free.

The divine ecologists are better known to us as the saints and mystics, prophets and spiritual teachers who have come throughout the ages. They themselves have become pure and free of all that pollutes the soul, and they are able to free others as well. They have liberated their souls from the limits of the physical body and have soared above on the pure, divine stream back to God.

Saints and mystics can hear the cries of the souls yearning to be free. They can show us our true nature. They teach us how to analyze ourself so that we can separate our soul or self from the layers of mind, matter, and illusion that cover it. They do this by teaching a method of meditation.

ఌ

## Preserving the Natural Beauty of the Soul

The fourth aspect of inner ecology is preserving the natural beauty of the soul. Once we have a direct experience of the inner Light and Sound, we realize that we are not the body but are soul. We realize that there is a higher Reality within us. It is the beginning of our journey to our true Home.

Spiritual adepts teach us those practices which will help us clean off the grime of ages. There are two things which will help to purify us faster: the cleansing water of Naam and ethical living.

Once we are taught the method of meditation and are given a contact with the Light and Sound of God, we need to engage in the inner practices every day. We need to set aside daily some time from our workaday life to commune with the current of Light and Sound within. The more we see and listen to the inner Light and Sound, the more our soul is cleansed, and the worldly impressions are washed away.

The second helping factor they teach us is to lead an ethical life. In order to progress on our spiritual journey within, we need to overcome anger, lust, greed, attachment, and ego. These are the five pollutants that cover the purity of the soul. They drag our attention into the world. If we analyze these five negative traits, we find they are all motivated by our desire for transitory and worldly pleasures. For example, we become angry when anything interferes with attaining our worldly desires. Lust is caused by the desire to gratify our senses. Greed results from our insatiable desire to amass either possessions, riches, and power, or name and fame. When we attain any of these we become attached to them and forget the spiritual values and our spiritual nature. Ego arises from pride of our transitory attainments: pride of wealth, worldly knowledge, and power.

To help us overcome these five negative qualities, we need to review our thoughts, words, and deeds each day. This gives us a realistic picture of the pollutants which defile the soul. We can then resolve to improve the following day.

Spiritual adepts lay great emphasis on ethical living and speak of it as a stepping-stone to spirituality. Sant Kirpal Singh used to say that it is difficult to become a human being in the true sense; but once we have accomplished this, it is relatively easy to find God. What is required is nothing short of the total transformation of one's life.

If our planet, with its interdependent ecological systems, is to survive, we have to learn to live in harmony with all creation. If we are polluting our world it means that we do not care about anyone else. If we cared about our family, if we cared about our neighbor, we would not do anything to pollute the environment and make life difficult for other human beings. The whole ecological problem could be solved if we as humans start to realize that each form of creation inhabiting the earth is an embodied soul. If we realize that the soul in us is the same soul that inhabits every being, whether plant or animal, and comes from the same Source, from the same Oversoul, from God, then we would care about and love every being. We would see the Light of God in each living thing. And what does love mean? Love means actually caring about someone else. Love does not mean just a physical attraction. The real divine love, really having love for someone, means you care about that person. And caring about someone means that you do not want to make his or her life difficult. If all of us in this world would start thinking of everyone else as our brothers and sisters, as being of the same essence as God that we are, then we would not do anything to harm other people. We would try to live our lives so that we do not pollute the environment in which other people have to live. Through the process of connecting ourselves to the Light and Sound of God, we begin to realize the Light of God in all beings and we start believing in the brotherhood of humanity and the Fatherhood of God. Once we attain that state, it reflects in our own lives and helps the society and the country in which we live and the whole world.

We have to develop a kind of respect for our environment in which we do not ignore the claims and contributions of even the tiniest of creatures. Ecologists are sensitive enough to avoid altering anything in the environ-ment which will upset the balance of nature. Similarly, when we advance spiritually, we begin to move through life with sensitivity. We no longer injure the feelings of others. We treat those with whom we come in contact with love and gentleness. As we develop the positive virtues and continue meditating on the Holy Naam, we will find that the imperfections and pollutants that covered us will fall away and we are restored to our original purity.

Dedicated ecologists feel a great sense of duty to work towards preserving the purity of the environment. They want to do what they can to live in harmony with nature. Similarly, those who discover themselves and realize God also feel a sense of responsibility. The attainment of the spiritual riches is not an end in itself. One develops a deep love for all creation. One sees the hand of God behind every blade of grass. This respect and love for life manifests itself in selfless service.

Those who realize God do not leave the world to spend it in isolated meditation. They develop an innate desire to serve their fellow beings, and all life. This may come as a surprise to many in the West who think that spirituality is life-negating and meant for recluses and monks. Sant Darshan Singh used to term that approach as "negative mysticism." He coined the term "positive mysticism." This approach means that while pursuing our spiritual goals, we continue to perform our obligations to our family, community, nation, and the world, and we do so to the best of our ability. We continue to earn our livelihood honestly so we can maintain ourselves and our family and can help those in need. We remain in the religion into which we are born, but live up to its true purpose – knowing ourselves and realizing God. We raise our families and see that they receive the best educational opportunities in life. We try to attain the best of both worlds. We strive to excel in all our endeavors. While living and working in the world, though, we are always mindful of our spiritual goal.

Let us devote our time to the spiritual practices so we can recover our innate God-given beauty. Once we develop it, we will reflect that radiance to all those with whom we come in contact. We will, in fact, shower that love on all living things and on our planet earth.

By restoring the ecological health of our soul, we will be purifying and uplifting all creation. Then, this world will return to the divine stage of godly bliss and ecstasy for which we were created.

Let me conclude with some verses from the poem, *The Cry of the Soul*, written by Sant Darshan Singh:

*We are but drops of the same fountain of divine beauty,*
*We are but waves on the great river of love.*

*We are diverse blossoms in the Garden of the Lord,*
*We have gathered in the same Valley of Light.*

*We who dwell on this earth belong to one humanity,*
*There is but one God, and we are all His children.*

# EXERCISE

Observe your own view on ecology. Try to add practices to your daily life that promote ecological balance.

Think about the ecology of the soul. What factors pollute the purity of soul? Make action plans, using this chapter, to eliminate those factors from your life.

# SEVENTEEN

# Spiritual Fulfillment in Modern Life

People all over the world are searching for the solutions to the mysteries of life and death and to find out what lies beyond this physical world. Current books, magazine articles, and conferences show that interest in spiritual pursuits is growing. More and more people want to learn how to achieve inner peace through spiritual experiences.

In modern life we find it hard to strike a happy medium in the development of our spiritual, intellectual, and physical sides. The pressures of life force us to give more weight to our intellectual growth, for that is what counts in our school career and in finding a good job. Our physical side is considered to be important for good health. We value exercise and sports for our physical and mental well-being. Health experts today are pointing out how physical exercise also relieves stress.

Thus, modern society as a whole values intellectual and physical growth. Unfortunately, it does not place a high value on spiritual development. We are brought up to associate spirituality with the rites and rituals of our religious institutions. If people tell us they are searching for God, we equate them with monks in a monastery sitting on wooden benches and praying day and night. In the past, people would leave their homes and their families to search for God in the forests or deserts. But the industrial and technological ages have made such demands upon humanity that people cannot abandon the world to pursue spirituality.

The challenge I would like to address is: How can we pursue spirituality in the setting of modern life? How can we search for God in a way that is socially acceptable and socially responsible? How can we attain spiritual heights without sacrificing our intellectual and physical growth? And how can we do so in the context of our family and community life?

Many people in the West are under the misconception that those who search for God must leave their homes and society and live in the jungles or on the mountaintops. Perhaps it was possible in the past, before we had such an interdependent economic system. But in today's world who can support themselves, not to mention their families, without holding jobs and contributing to society?

### ❧

## Positive Mysticism

We can attain self-knowledge and God-realization in the context of modern life. We can lead a productive, fulfilling life in the world while working towards spiritual ends. Sant

Darshan Singh called this approach "positive mysticism." This was opposed to "negative mysticism" which required one to give up the world in order to find God. The path of positive mysticism enables one to achieve the best of both the worlds. The concept of positive mysticism can give us an understanding of how we can achieve spiritual growth while meeting the challenges of the age.

Spiritual development is a process by which we attain self-knowledge and God-realization. We have a physical body, and we have a mind and intellect. Spiritual growth involves the realization that we are not the body and the mind, but in reality we are soul. Throughout our lives we have become so identified with our body and mind that on our own we cannot separate our true self from them. In fact, the great teachers of ancient Greece exhorted us to do so with the words "Know Thyself." This expression is written on the entrance to the temple of the Delphic Oracle.

Spiritual teachers who have mastered the art of knowing themselves can teach others how to achieve this goal. If we look at the various methods used throughout history, we find that the most effective way to realize our self is through meditation. Saints, seers, and mystics have told us that God is within. They further explain that soul is a part of God. If we can turn our attention from the world outside to the inner realms we will find that we are soul and will realize God who is within us. We will experience ourselves as soul, separate from the body. We will experience the exhilaration of being free from the bodily cage, and we will soar like a bird through higher and higher realms of consciousness.

Words are inadequate to describe the intoxication and

thrill of the higher realms. We see vistas of beauty beyond any we can dream of in this world. But nothing can compare with the absolute bliss our soul experiences when it reunites with the Creator. When our soul reaches its ultimate goal, it merges back into its source. God is the source of all love, the source of all bliss. When the soul merges back in Him, the two become one. We enter a state of eternal and lasting happiness and love. This is the highest goal of our meditations. The beauty of the meditation process is that these experiences stay with us forever. After meditation, the soul returns to the body and it carries with it the intoxication and bliss from its sojourn in the beyond.

This process of meditation can be practiced in the comfort of our own home, while sitting in a train on the way to work, or in any moment of solitude. It involves no difficult practice, no rigorous postures. We can meditate when sitting in any pose that is most convenient and in which we can sit still for a period of time. Meditation on the inner Light and Sound is so simple that it can be practiced by a young child or an elderly person, by those who are healthy and those who have physical disabilities.

After finding a comfortable position, one closes one's eyes, gazes within, and experiences, through the help of a teacher, the divine Light and Sound. As we can see, this process does not require us to sit on a mountaintop or in a jungle. It can be done in our home and society.

## Meditation and Modern Life

By practicing meditation for an hour or two every day, we will find great rewards and benefits. First, our concentration naturally improves. By meditating, we develop more sustained concentration. This can be applied to our workaday life. We can use our concentration to develop our intellectual faculties. We develop an increased attention span which will help us learn and absorb more information. While most people are so distracted that they only absorb partial information from what they read and hear, meditation helps us absorb more and retain more.

Through meditation, we also experience physical well-being. During meditation our body is relaxed. We are free from stress and tension. Medical doctors have discovered the effects of stress on our physical health. There are many diseases related to stress. By meditating, we relieve our stress and tensions. The more we come in contact with the inner realms and experience the joy within, the more we carry that joy with us in our daily life. Meditation helps us face many of life's problems with a calmer, more relaxed attitude. Having experienced the worlds beyond, we know that the problems of this transitory world are ephemeral. We know of a higher reality and can look at the world's difficulties with a different perspective. While we still must pass through the trials and tribulations of life, we have so much inner support and inner strength that we do not experience their pinching effects.

This increase in concentration and control over stress and tension will help us achieve success in our worldly activities. A natural by-product is that we will be more efficient and more productive in our places of work. I have personally seen people suddenly shoot up to the top of their fields after practicing meditation for a number of years. They soon outshone the other employees because of their increased concentration. They were able to produce more in less time than those who had not developed the art of concentration.

Meditation helps students excel in their studies. Students are also able to concentrate longer and retain more information. Again, I have seen many young people who had been practicing meditation rise to the top of their class. We all know that those students who do well will be in a better position to attain the best jobs and career opportunities.

There is yet another aspect of meditation which will have untold benefits in our lives. As the soul journeys into the beyond and experiences its relationship with God it has a great realization. It sees each living thing, whether human, animal, or plant, as a part of God. It sees that there is a soul in every living thing. Once we experience that we are all a part of God, we begin to see God's Light shining in all. We see all creation as children of the one Parent. This is a profound realization that brings about fundamental changes in the way we live. We develop love for everyone and every living creature. We begin to love all people equally and consider them part of our own family. We develop tolerance and patience towards those around us. We develop the sublime qualities of compassion and understanding. We want to help others in need. A great transformation takes place in us, and we radiate love and sympathy to everyone around us.

The more we perfect our meditations, the more we come in contact with the source of love within, and the more we love and are loved by others. We will find that the things that upset us before no longer have any sway over us. Peace and harmony will enter our hearts and homes. Our family and social life will become peaceful and blissful.

One of the greatest benefits of meditation is that we will not only have peace in our own homes, but will contribute to the peace of the world. Throughout the world, people are praying for peace. But, as the expression goes, charity begins at home. World peace can only become a reality when each of us individually has peace in our own circles. If we bring peace into our individual spheres, the effect will be cumulative, and it will contribute to world peace.

### ✌

## Positive Contribution to Society

Spirituality is an active path. We become more involved in the betterment of our world. Positive mysticism means that while pursuing spiritual progress, we also make a positive contribution to our family, society, and the world at large.

Part of our spiritual growth is the development of ethical virtues. By becoming a noble and virtuous person, we stand as a pillar of strength and inspiration to those around us. By meditating and developing love for all, we spread a divine fragrance wherever we go. We feel moved by the suffering of others and are quick to help those in need. In whatever sphere we are working we become a source of help to those around us. We try to utilize our talents for the good of humanity. Sant Kirpal Singh visited the sick in the hospitals and in their homes. He helped many people in need. Sant Darshan Singh also helped those in need as well as victims of natural disasters such as famine, flood, earthquakes and volcanos, providing them with assistance, medical care, and clothing. He himself was a living example of positive mysticism, and there is much we can learn from his example.

If we are sincerely interested in knowing our selves, the means of doing so are available. We will be performing the greatest service to our own self by developing spiritually, and we will become a positive force in the lives of our family, friends, co-workers, and the world. We will find the perfect balance in our lives as we develop body, mind, and spirit. By practicing positive mysticism we can successfully meet the challenge of the age.

## EXERCISE

Make an action plan to incorporate spirituality into your life. Make a daily time chart of your schedule. Schedule time for introspection of your self in regard to thoughts, words, and deeds that hinder your spiritual progress. Then, schedule time for meditation and selfless service each day.

# EIGHTEEN

# Inner and Outer Peace

*T*hroughout the world, we find people have many ways of expressing their desire for peace. We hear phrases such as "peace be with you." At Christmas, people send greeting cards or sing songs about "peace on Earth." We find that people will hold up two fingers in the form of a "V" which symbolizes "peace." When someone dies, we pray that he or she "rests in peace."

Nations meet continually to search for ways to make peace with each other. Organizations dedicated to peace have sprung up in many countries. There is even a Nobel peace prize for individual contributions to this noble cause.

The quest for peace is universal. In every age and in every country, people have been trying to find peace within their environment, within their societies, and within the world. It is strange that this search has been going on for so long and has been sought by so many people, yet its attainment remains elusive. Few find peace for themselves. Nothing on earth seems to provide us with a true and lasting peace. We start to wonder why peace is so hard to achieve.

❧

## Why Peace Is So Elusive

First, we should analyze what peace is. A dictionary defines it as freedom from strife, and a state of serenity and calmness. Inherent in this definition is the answer to why peace is so difficult to find. Life and strife seem to go hand in hand. Whether one is rich or poor, a king or a peasant, one's life is always beset with one problem or another.

There is a story from the life of Lord Buddha which aptly illustrates this truth. A woman whose young son had died approached Lord Buddha. She was shedding copious tears over the loss of her child. She asked Buddha to help bring her son back to life and ease the terrible pain in her heart. Buddha, in his wisdom, told her he would help her if she could first bring back the mustard seed from a household in which no one ever died. The lady followed his instructions and moved from one home to the next. Yet, at each door, she received the same reply. She realized that there wasn't any family that could pass through life escaping the loss of one of its members.

Death is the one inevitable fact of life. Sickness and disease are yet others. We need only examine our own life to see how difficult it is to go through one's existence without any mishap, accident, or illness. Medical books are filled with numerous diseases that can afflict human beings.

There is no dearth of accidents that could befall us as we move through life's highways and byways. With death or illness hanging over our heads, it is difficult to live in perpetual, uninterrupted peace.

Even if our physical body is fairly healthy, few can pass through life without any strife. There are many occurrences that produce stress. If we have a family, we know that the illness, unhappiness, or misfortune of any member causes the others to be distressed. Whenever any two people live or work together, there are bound to be tensions due to differences of opinions or differing viewpoints. There are a host of other problems that afflict our lives. If we search for peace in our outer life, at best we can find transitory moments. We certainly do have times in which we enjoy the warmth of being with our loved ones, or we have moments of happiness from some gain or achievement. But these moments are fleeting. Inevitably, life again comes with its panorama of problems. The great mystic-poet saint, Sant Darshan Singh, expressed this beautifully in one of his verses:

*Whenever your devotee's condition alters but a little,*
*Life presents itself to me with another cup of sorrow.*

It seems as if lasting peace in this life is virtually impossible. Life is more like a pendulum in which we swing back and forth from moments of joy to moments of sorrow.

### Attaining Inner Peace

But true peace can be attained in this lifetime. We only need to undergo a paradigm shift. Our angle of vision needs to be changed. We normally look for peace in the outer world. We hope to find it in our possessions, positions, and relationships. But the loss of any of these causes us to become agitated and distraught. Our peace of mind is disturbed. There is a way to have true peace. Just as Birbal shortened Akbar's line by drawing a longer line next to it, the solution to finding peace can be found in a similar way. We cannot change the nature of the world and its problems. But we can add a new dimension to life that will give us peace.

Peace can be found within us. Many people believe the outer world is the only reality. But the enlightened luminaries throughout history have had mystical experiences which verified for them the existence of inner spiritual regions.

Buddha found enlightenment by inverting within himself. Christ has said, "The Kingdom of heaven is within you." The Muslim and the Judeo-Christian scriptures speak of the contact that the prophets had with God. Mystics in every religion have described their inner spiritual experiences. These higher realms co-exist simultaneously with us in the physical world. They are realms of eternal peace and bliss. We cannot change the world, but we can tune into those realms lying within us. By doing so we will change our perspective in our life.

The way to reach this inner world is through meditation. Meditation is the process by which we separate our soul from the body to voyage into the regions within. Spiritual teachers or mystics who have mastered this science can teach it to us. First, they explain the theory so we can understand the process. Then, they give us a practical demonstration of it through meditation on the inner Light and Sound.

The more we come in contact with the Light and Sound, the more bliss we experience. The soul experiences pure joy and happiness. This bliss stays with the soul throughout the day and night, and we experience peace and contentment.

**❧**

## Contributing to Outer Peace

By mastering meditation under the guidance of a spiritual teacher, we not only attain personal fulfillment, but we become an instrument for bringing peace and joy to those around us. When we merge in the Creator, we recognize that all living things are children of God. We realize that the Light of God that is within us is within everyone else. We realize that all beings are brothers and sisters in the Creator. It is at this stage that we develop true love for all, for our fellow beings, and for all creation. We become ambassadors of God's love. We radiate love to others. If each person had this realization, there would be true peace on this planet.

By experiencing inner peace, we can achieve outer peace. By entering into the sanctuary of peace within us, we gain the inner treasures. Some people may feel that the path of meditation is one of escapism. They feel that it requires one to sit in an outer cave or on a mountaintop like a recluse. But meditation does not lead to escapism; rather, it makes us more alive. It is one of the most effect-ive ways to actively work towards outer peace. We should maintain a balanced life in the world. While attending to our spiritual progress, we should also lead a normal life, fulfilling our worldly responsibilities. We need to work in the world to earn a living. We must care for our family. We should contribute to the needs of our neighbors, our community, our society, the nation, and the world. Whatever we undertake, we should do to the best of our capabilities.

The spiritual path is twofold. We achieve inner enlightenment and peace for ourselves. Then, we use our talents and skills and the gift of our human life to make the world a better place, a more peaceful place. If we are a doctor, we should be the best possible doctor. If we are a carpenter, we should be the best carpenter. If we are a musician, we should be the best musician we can. In this way, we make improvements in our society and make life better for all around us. By developing our inner and our outer life, we will become complete human beings. We will find fulfillment and peace for ourselves and help others achieve it as well.

We may not be able to change our life or eliminate its problems, but through meditation we can look at it differently. Through meditation we can face life because we understand it better. We have the knowledge to help us face up to what happens to us with strength. We will have gained the inner peace that comes from spiritual consciousness. And we will be a source of peace to all around us.

It is my hope and prayer that each one of you experiences this inner peace and in this way contributes to the peace of the world.

## EXERCISE

Observe the state of outer peace in your environment. Note conflicts and issues that arise. Continue to practice meditation and personal transformation in your daily life. Try to become a positive influence on the people in your environment by maintaining your own peace. Avoid telling others what to do. Be peaceful yourself, radiate peace, and observe the contribution you make to world peace.

# About the Author:

Sant Rajinder Singh Ji Maharaj is one of the world's leading experts in meditation. He is author of *Inner and Outer Peace through Meditation* (with a Foreword by H.H. the Dalai Lama), *Empowering Your Soul through Meditation, Spiritual Pearls for Enlightened Living,* and *Silken Thread of the Divine.* He has presented his powerful, yet simple technique of meditation to millions of people throughout the world through seminars, meditation retreats, conferences, books, hundreds of magazine articles, television and radio shows, CD's, DVD's, and Internet broadcasts. His method of achieving inner and outer peace through meditation has been recognized and highly respected by civic, religious, and spiritual leaders wherever he goes. He teaches a non-denominational meditation that can be practiced by people of all cultures, religions, ages, and walks of life.

His other books include: *Spiritual Thirst, Echoes of the Divine, Vision of Spiritual Unity and Peace, Ecology of the Soul and Positive Mysticism, Education for a Peaceful World,* and in Hindi, *Spirituality in Modern Times, Self Realization, Search for Peace within the Soul, Salvation through Naam, Spiritual Treasures, Experience of the Soul, Spiritual Talks,* and *True Happiness.* His books have been translated into fifty languages.

He convened many International Human Unity Conferences, attended by world religious, civic, and social leaders, held in Delhi, India; Bogota, Colombia; Munich, Germany; Lima, Peru; San Juan, Puerto Rico; and Santo Domingo, Dominican Republic. He was president of the 7th World Religions Conference, and was a major presenter at the Parliament of World Religions held in Chicago in 1993. He also convenes annual conferences on Human Integration and on Global Mysticism. He led a meditation for thousands of people at the 50th Anniversary of the United Nations held in New York.

Sant Rajinder Singh Ji is head of Science of Spirituality, a nonprofit, nondenominational organization, with centers in over forty countries throughout North America, Central and South America, Europe, Asia, Africa, Australia, and Oceania. Science of Spirituality provides a forum for people to learn meditation, experience personal transformation, and bring about inner and outer peace.

Sant Rajinder Singh Ji has been honored with numerous awards and tributes, including a Peace Award. He is active in helping humanity. His organization, Science of Spirituality, has provided assistance to people who underwent natural disasters such as the volcano in Colombia, the earthquake in Mexico, floods in Delhi, and the hurricane in Florida. In 2001, following the earthquake in Gujarat which left over a half million people homeless, his organization provided aid to the devastated areas and rebuilt an entire village, including all the homes, a community building/meditation hall, a school and medical dispensary. Science of Spirituality raised and donated money to victims of Hurricane Katrina and for the Tsumani disaster in Asia, including building three schools for the victims of the Tsunami disaster.

Sant Rajinder Singh Ji Maharaj can be contacted at Science of Spirituality, 4 S. 175 Naperville Rd., Naperville, Illinois 60563: Tele: (630) 955-1200; or Fax: (630) 955-1205, or Kirpal Ashram, Sant Kirpal Singh Marg, Vijay Nagar, Delhi, India 110009; Tele: 91-11-27117100 or Fax: 91-11-27214040.

For more information, contact: Radiance Publishers, 1042 Maple Ave.

Lisle, IL 60532.

To order books, call: (630) 577-7624
or email: sales@radiancepublishers.com

Website: www.radiancepublishers.com

JUN − 5 2014

CPSIA information can be obtained at www.ICGtesting.com
Printed in the USA
LVOW12s2239050514

384571LV00012B/234/P